OverHeads

By Tj. Aitken

Published By Novus Resource Inc. a Michigan Corporation
ISBN 9781518733611

For Victoria
And all who suffer from Chronic Lyme Disease

OverHeads
Tj. Aitken

In hundreds of tribal rituals from cultures and regions throughout history we see representations of faces as sculptures to convey something about a deity. The mask is often used in ceremony to magnify and animate a deity or a story concept. Conversations about spiritual conditions are in disfavor currently yet we have very deep connections in many ways to ideas, groups, things, and activities that supplant spiritual ritual yet really become worship. Our gods (small g) are many, and we spend much energy deifying or placating them. We worship things like our cars, hobbies, bodies. We obsess over perceptions or group interactions. In modern industrial jargon an organization's knowledge or the capabilities and wisdom to excel at something, are all referred to as "Tribal Knowledge". When you work at a company you are a member of that tribe. If you are a connoisseur of wine, beer, fashion, or antiques you are members of those tribes. Sometimes we wear masks to hide our tribe, sometimes to exalt. When you suffer anxiety over your weight, what people think, or how tidy things are, these little demons have to be placated, just like cultures that believe demons will cause trouble unless offered something. We ritualize our placations as sure as the primitive who dances wearing a mask.

I collect 'like' objects that seem to have artistic character (like auto overhead consoles). My piling system of interesting materials includes upholstery fabric, car parts, metal bits and many other things. "Road feathers" are tire shards from the highway. These are interesting and often beautiful forms. They have their own narrative of intense processing of steel and rubber to be made into tough tires. Then they spin against roads for thousands of miles to be slowly worn down before the dramatic explosion and violent flapping that creates them. I choose road feathers for their intense story so related to our times. This body of artworks came from observations as I pondered my piles of objects and materials. I was combining and altering the overhead consoles and began to write down what these objects were saying to me from how they appeared. Each day's observations would feed the next move to make the works. The written statements became guides to material selections, additions, subtractions and general manipulations that forged these works. The essays are now a part of each piece and in many ways more important than the sculptures.

There is a great deal of overhead in a modern life. How much is really necessary?
I believe healthy spiritual awareness can be negated by the noise of all this "Overhead".

The works in this book were originally a tithe during a time of transition from industry to fine art. The intent was to spend time in prayer and meditation while I readied the studio for the business of full time sculpture. I had works going in many veins but this was a pause and a reflection period to deepen a spiritual relationship.

Most of these pieces were completed in 2005/6 and readied for an exhibition by early 2007. A few came a bit later as solutions arose to starts from the original period. Some have been destroyed by nature, a few were sold.

When Chronic Lyme Disease struck our family and the need to raise funds for medical bills became pressing, the OverHeads were called up as an offering to those who might help with the cause. This book was started in 07 and completed in late 15 for dedication to all who suffer from this illness. Give a copy to a friend and help a person who wears a fairly normal mask on the outside but who's insides are more like these images, calling out in pain, dizzy and afflicted with anomalies that are grievous. Americans seem OK but we suffer spiritual conditions that should be unmasked.

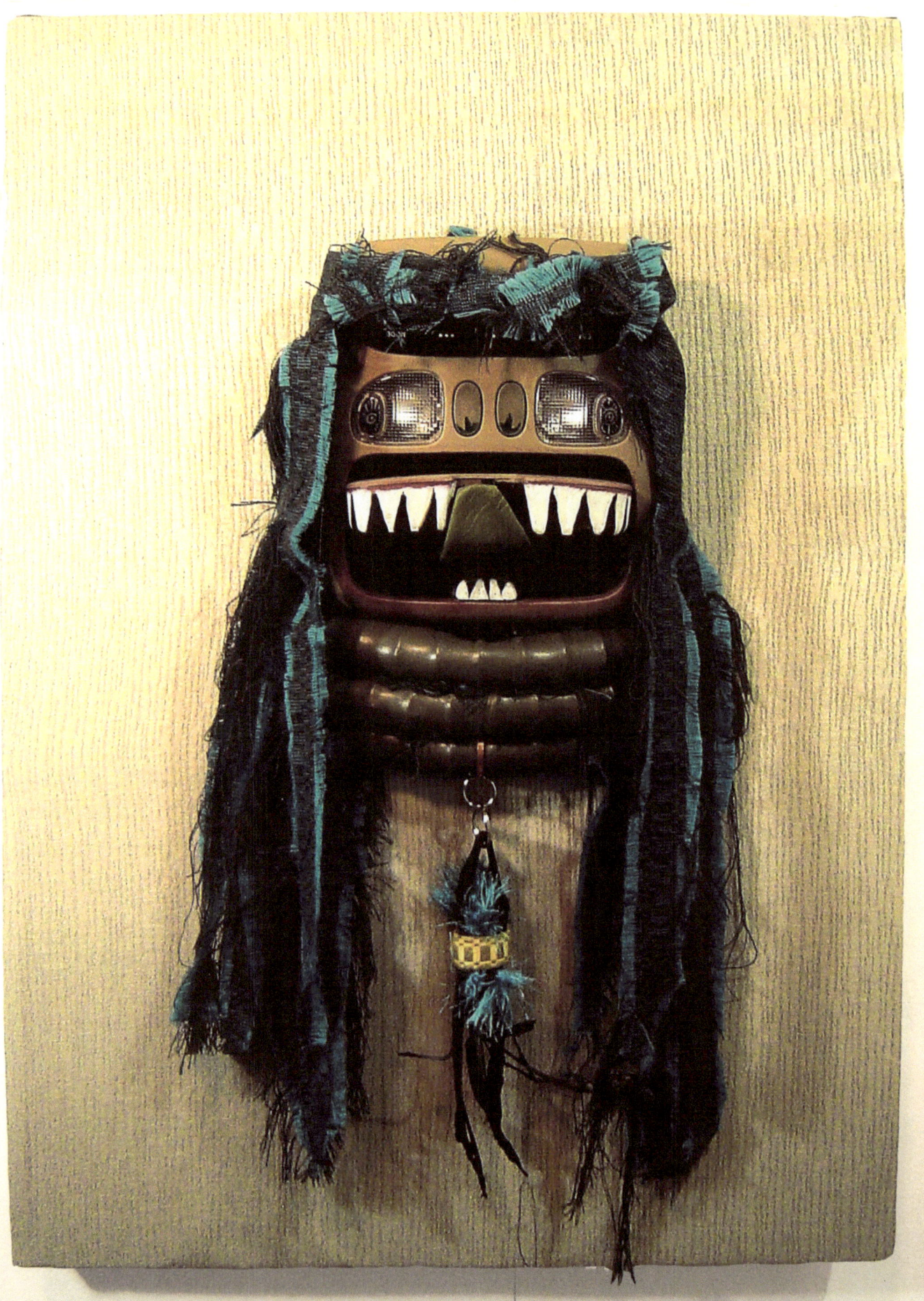

Green Gossip

Envy, just green with it. That is how we find ourselves so often.
It will sometimes drive us to spread gossip about others, a bit of sabotage for the competition. Oh, the tainted and spoiled spirit that can manifest from our comparison to others. And oddly enough it goes on in every single strata of society, from the least to the mighty, from the toddler to the old miser. Rock stars not happy with a recording selling three million when another sells ten. Have you ever gone into prayer with a supplication for more, born of a mere desire to compete? What debts have we accumulated simply because we must keep up with the Joneses?

Pride and envy can produce a wagging tongue that is as green as the bacteria that inhabit a stagnant swamp. And if it is rolling off our tongue imagine just how much must be on the mind, and how deep the furrows in the cortex that these impulses travel.

Proverbs 26:22
The words of a gossip are like choice morsels; they go down to a man's inmost parts.
26:20
Without wood a fire goes out; without gossip a quarrel dies down.

What's in your worship?

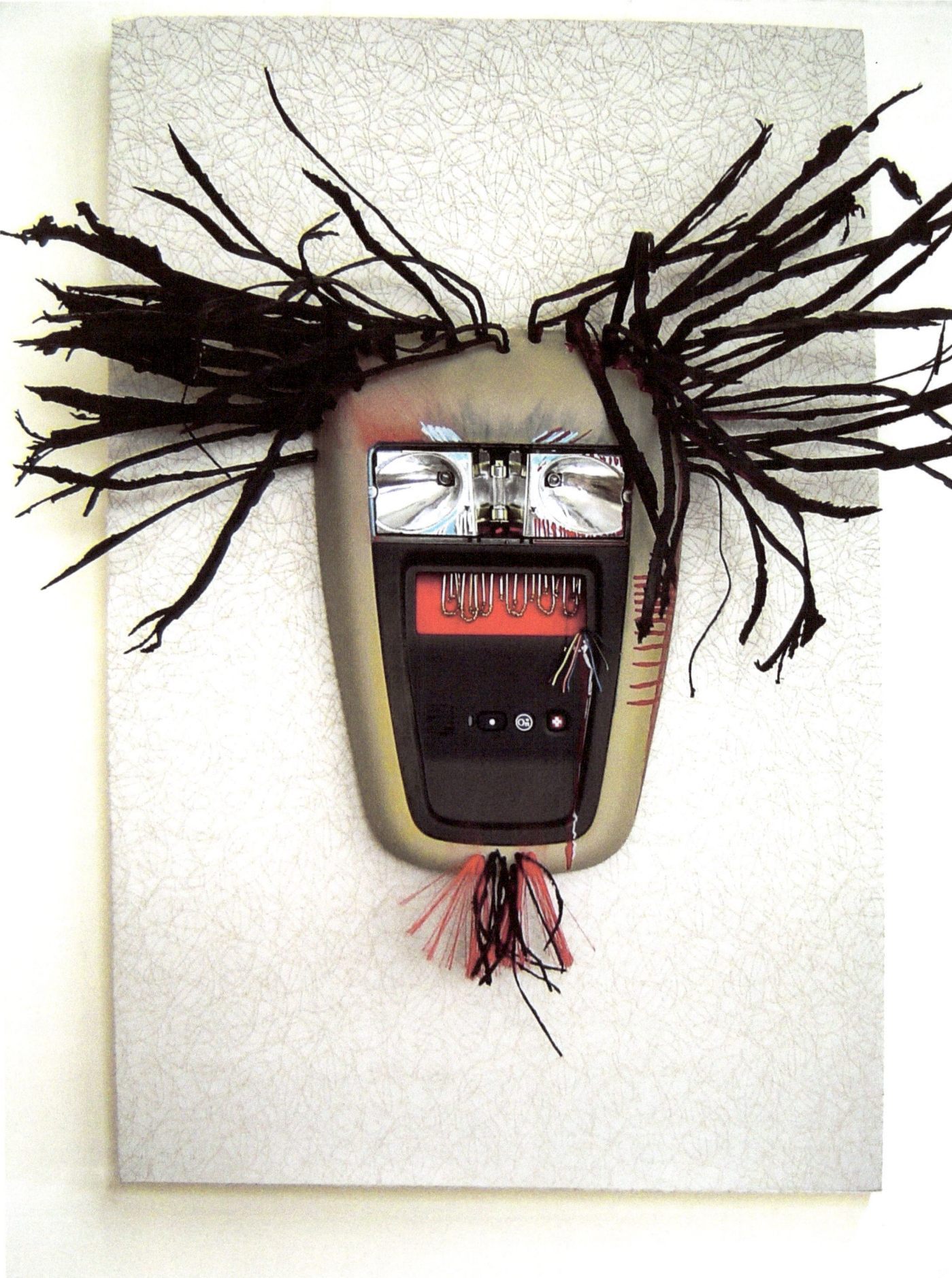

Cool Daddio

      Are we cool enough?   Are we under control, suave and debonair? Do we rank with the "in" crowd far above the losers? Man, it is in our style, our dress, our talk, our crowd. This awareness comes in puberty and in many, just takes over everything. Some of us never grow out of it's domination. We must be cool. And the act of pointing out the low status of another is like counting coo. It stimulates us and we believe we have achieved through these petty comments.   The concern about cool is probably the greatest distraction from a spiritual relationship ever conceived. It is elusive, fleeting, and indefinable, making it only achievable by those who truly believe they have it, confirmed by those around them aspiring to be there themselves.

      Cool can be a perfect mockery to the condition of righteousness, and a tremendous impediment to the ability to get close to a God who knows better of you and your state. The grand illusion of being cool deceives so many. Just look at the celebrity worship that the entertainment, and fashion industries receive. Yes we can be so cool, but what is in our worship? Can we be cool before God? Fat chance, and if we are focused on cool, then God is not in our consciousness. When we are cool our heart is cool, and warmth of heart is required to come to the presence of God. Ever loose your cool to get before God? But that brings another topic:

What's in your worship? Dude

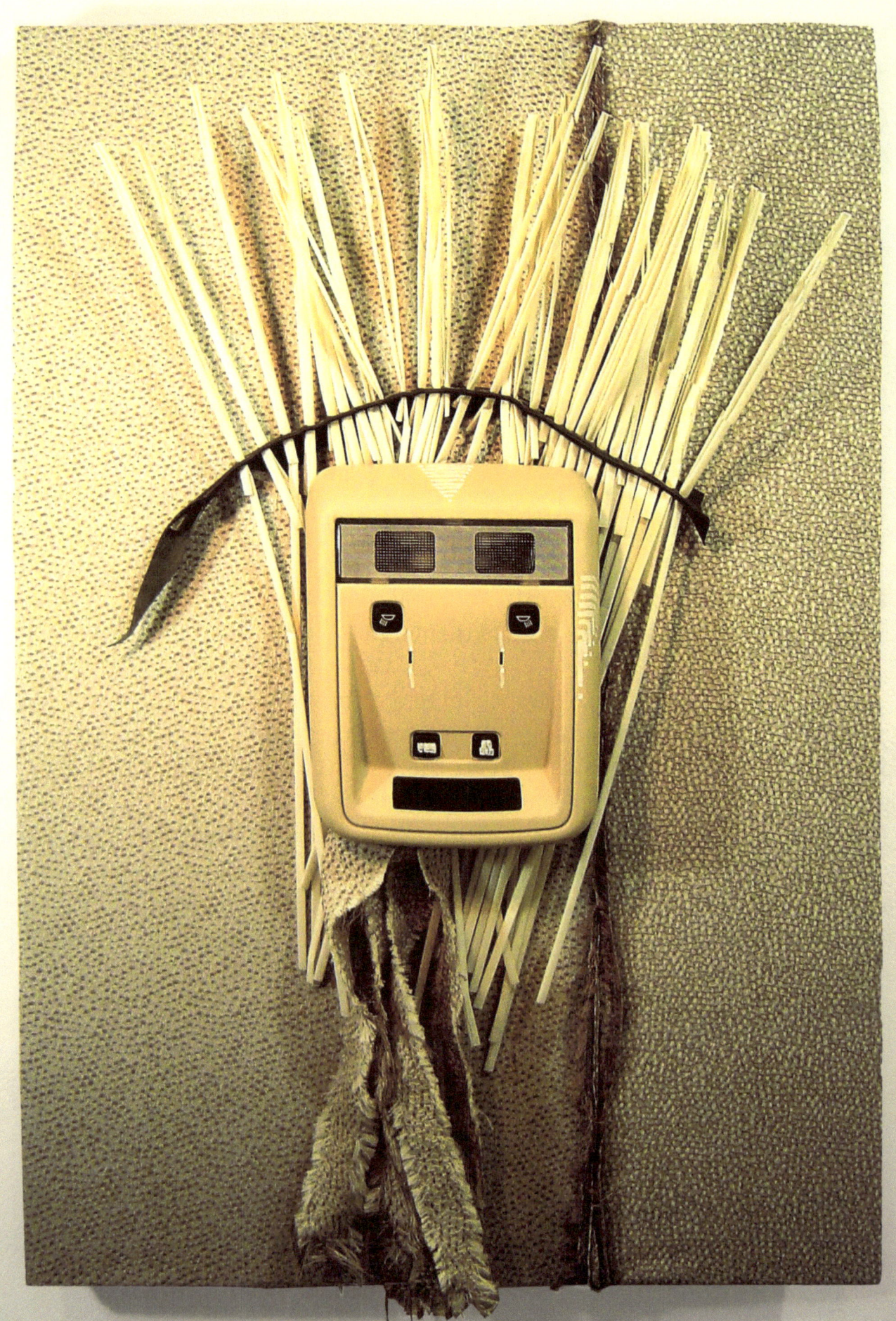

Spanking Clean

You know the room, it has white carpet, and white furniture possibly even with plastic covers. The walls are immaculate with carefully selected decorations. Yes, everything is perfectly dust free and practically sanitized like an operating room. Oddly enough this space is labeled a living room but so seldom does anyone go there that it bears no evidence of ever being lived in. Yes indeed it is spanking clean, by design and upkeep.

We often believe we must have a place like this to receive guests properly. After all, what would the neighbors say?

Have you ever mowed the lawn twice so the crisscross pattern is perfect? Have you spent time putting the contents of a cupboard into order by size? Have you contributed more money to your hair stylist than to, say, a missionary?

What happens when you want to receive the utmost of visitation? How can you prepare to receive the Holy Spirit of God and enter into worship in spirit and truth? The truth of the matter is, you will never scrub it clean enough, never get it straight and orderly enough, never ever produce an orderly organized self to God almighty! There is simply no cleanser no disinfectant that can provide a space appropriate for Him. Those who must chase dirt until the last molecule is purged do so in an endless futility. Prepare yourself for a visit from God? How? We cannot create a bubble of nice, when we live under a smokestack spewing soot all day. So we must just give in, come to the Christ who was provided for just this condition we hate. This state of unclean, that we can neither sponge or vacuum, replace or organize. It is simply tainted by the nature of our being here in this fallen world. Cleanliness is next to sinfulness, because the perfection of a loving God can not be approximated so, why try?

He has offered you a free coupon for a complete make-over, and frankly, you will never achieve it yourself. So take the deal. Give up your personal preparation, it'll never be ready.

What's in Your Worship?

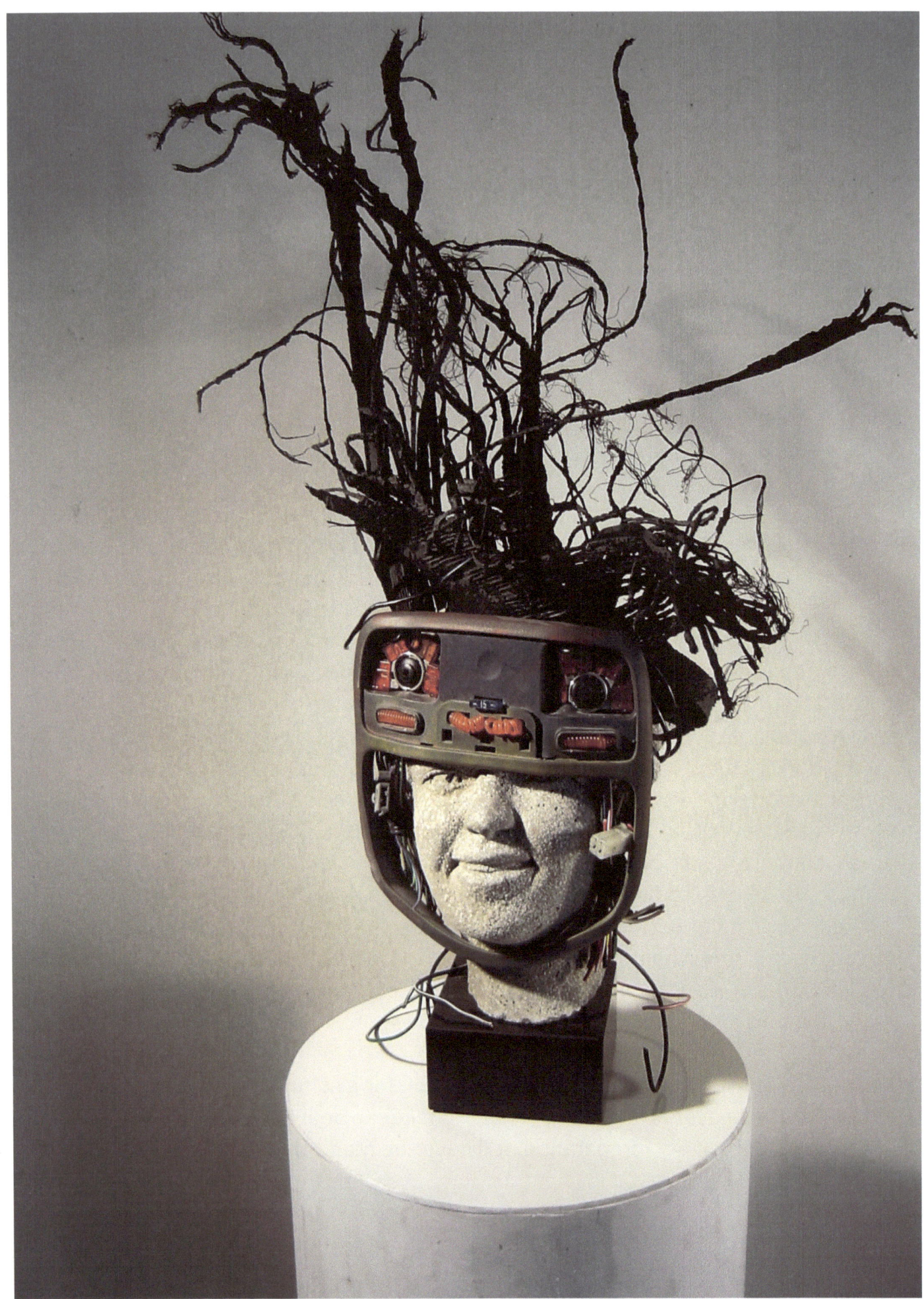

Inner Child

Who are we down deep? Same person we started out as, but hopefully wiser. Inside our masks of maturity lurks our inner child. A wonder filled, explorer who laughs easily but can be mischievous.   Yes we only let them out in small peaks, and only in front of those we really trust not to take advantage of our child state.

But growing wisdom also accumulates the jade barnacles of negative attitudes. Our encrustation of experience can crush new ideas and spiritual awakening. We are such skeptics. We hide the fact that we were young and stupid and now are just not so young anymore. But this also may hide us from the Master. A prerequisite for entry to His most extreme place of marvel rests in the way we enter.

Matt 18:3
I say unto you, except ye be converted, and become as little children, ye shall not enter into the kingdom of heaven.

Ah! mischief and all, a package of innocence must be dug out of its long lodging in pithy growth of years. Buried somewhere in your old body of flesh nests an inner child who must be nourished to the fore by exercises in humility. This is a tough one for the highly educated, the hard and bloodied fighters and the striving success stories of shrewd business, except maybe for the mischief.

Dare you bring that whelp forth?

What's in your Worship?

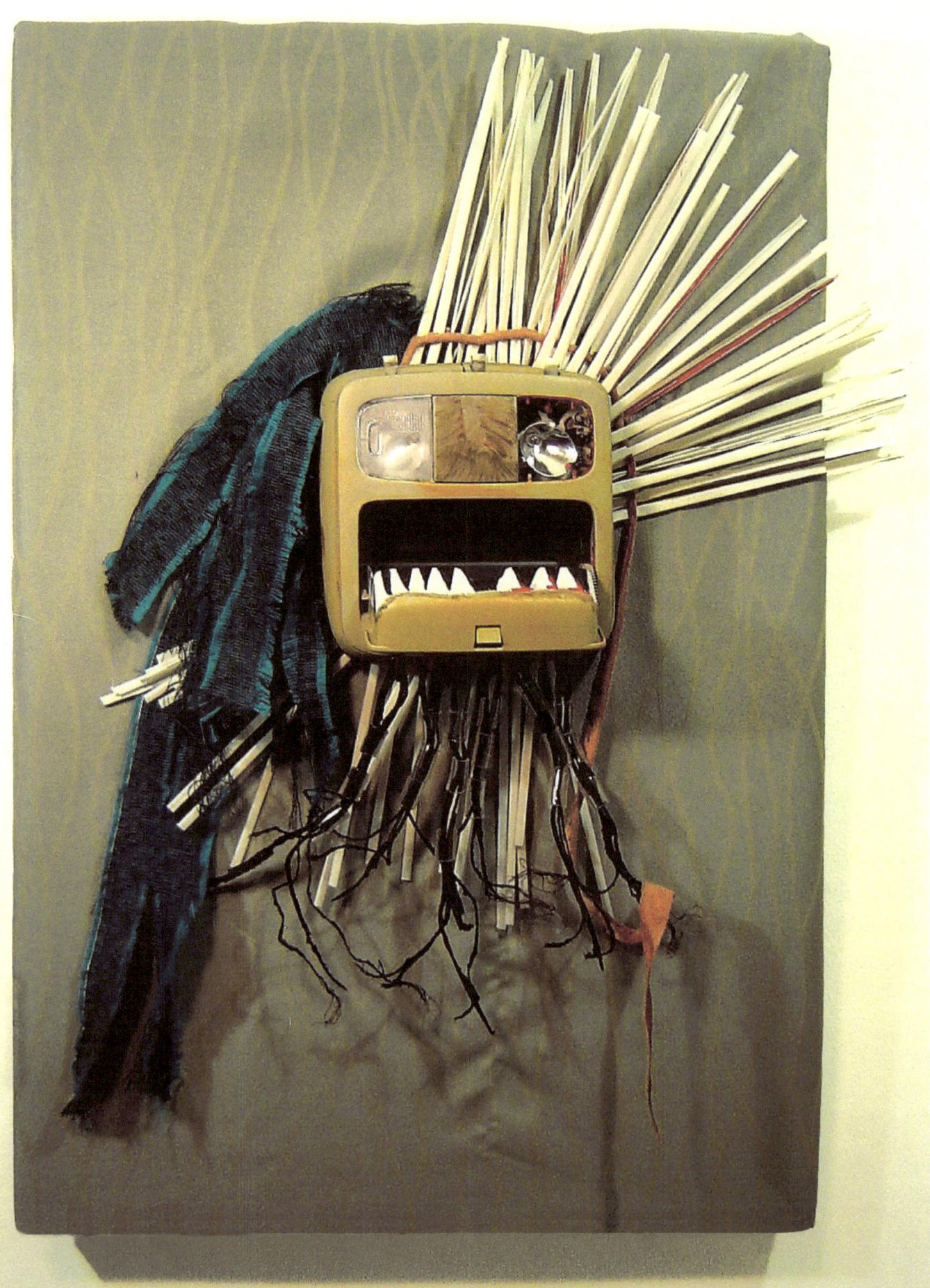

Mathew's Angst

They have been described as "the window to the soul" and there is truly a phenomena that telegraphs information about individuals when we look in their eyes. "Her eyes sparkled and shinned, like the stars" says the love struck, "He had Blood in his eye"- a phrase denoting one who wanted a fight. "You can't hide your lyin' eyes, and your smile is a thin disguise" song by the Eagles

Mathew 6: 22-24
The lamp of the body is the eye, if it is clear the body is full of light. But if the eye is bad your whole body is full of darkness. If the light in you is darkness then how great is the darkness.

Our world of distraction can lead us to total over-load. We just have so many things to think about, worry about. Our need to take action in so many directions can lead us to a virtual catatonic state, being frazzled, at the end of our rope. We can let the light in us fade like an old flashlight battery, we can burn it on unimportant concerns. And others can see it in our eyes. What is this energy? Where does it come from? In cartoons the dead are often depicted with just 'x's for eyes. The frail jewel of an eyeball in it's liquid envelope of tear can tell so much about the depth of life within. Not just the physical blood pumping and breath, but the state of the soul, the events that have shaped this life, the hope for the future, and the probable impact this individual could have on us. Consider this about the author of life:

John chapter 1:
"He was with God in the beginning. In him was life, and that life was the light of men. The light shines in the darkness, but the darkness has not understood it."

Our "countenance" comes through in our posture and in our eyes. If you are on the way to darkness it shows. We have so much to distract us these days from the true light of the world, we can get so concerned about this or that, that our light can get so very dim. And our ability to come to a spiritual relationship can be virtually gone. But then, when we enter into darkness we may cry out in anguish and there, in that despair, a living God will come to us. The light does shine in the darkness. Will you comprehend it? You must be willing to let the rest of those draining concerns go.

What's in Your Worship?

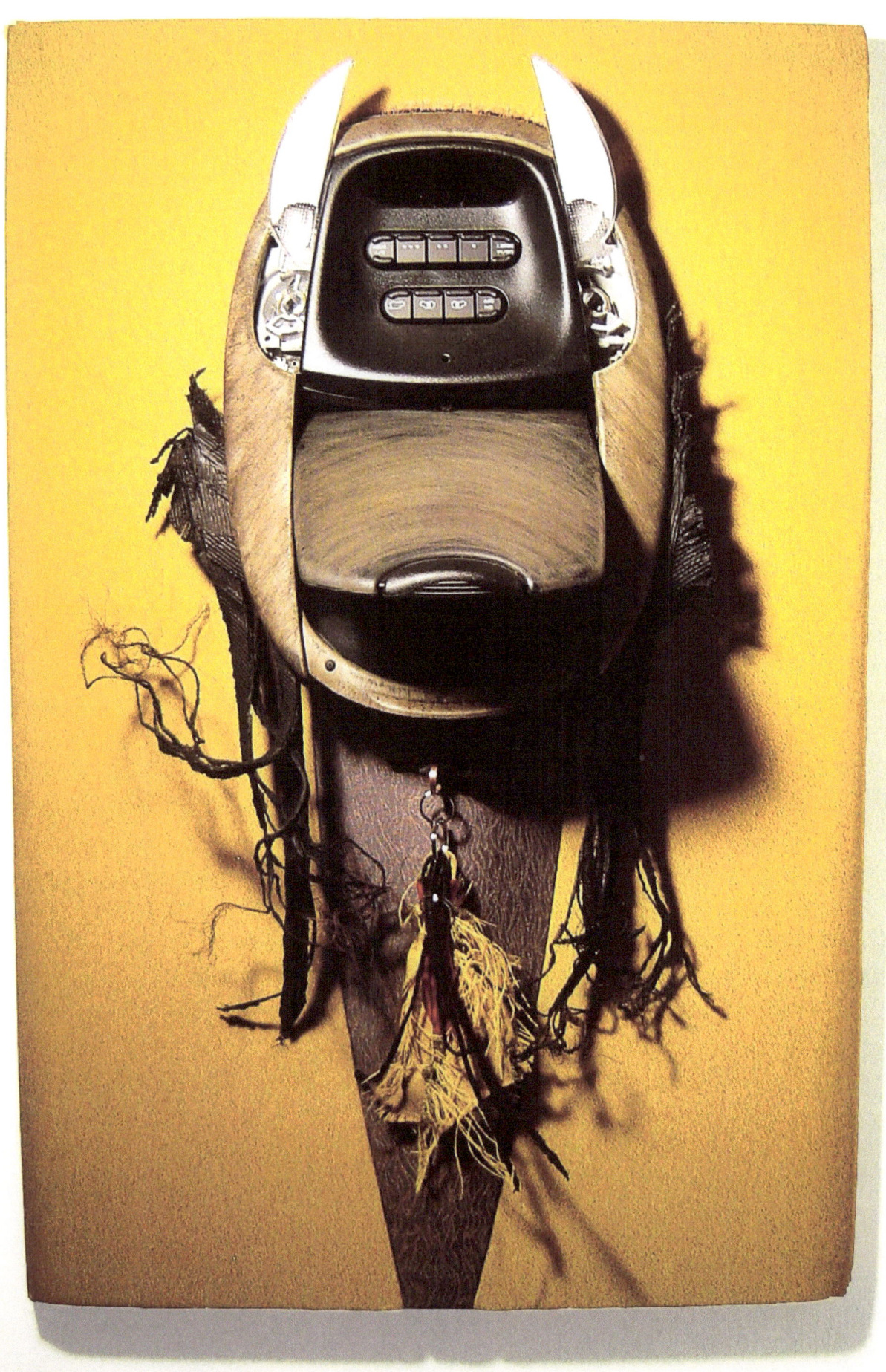

The Golden Calf

We revert to what we are familiar with under duress, or when we don't know what else to do. Consider the people who said:

"Come, make us gods who will go before us. As for this fellow Moses, we don't know what has happened to him." (Exodus 32:2)

They had seen the plagues in Egypt, they had experienced the Passover, they had witnessed the red sea part, and passed through. Now after a short wait for the spiritual message they give up and revert to what they knew, *demanding* that Aaron the priest make them a golden calf to worship.

What do you revel in? What gods go before you in your daily life? Cars, homes, Sports, Movies? We revert so quickly. Our rote response kicks in and we do what is practically a reflex. So often these things are so far from our real spiritual encounters that it is a wonder that the ten commandments survived at all.

In reviews of actual police shoot-outs where officers died, they found pockets full of casings. Precious seconds had been wasted in the heat of battle to pick up the empties, not because it was a good idea but because that is what they had done in training! (This practice was changed.) So what have you conditioned yourself to do? What is on your training table?

When we come to worship, and we seek to worship in spirit and truth, we may be under pressure that we are not used to. It may take longer to get it started than we had thought or planned for. The rest of our life enters in at these points and we revert to what we know. *"We don't know what became of that guy who went up the mountain, let's do what we always did."*

What's in your worship?

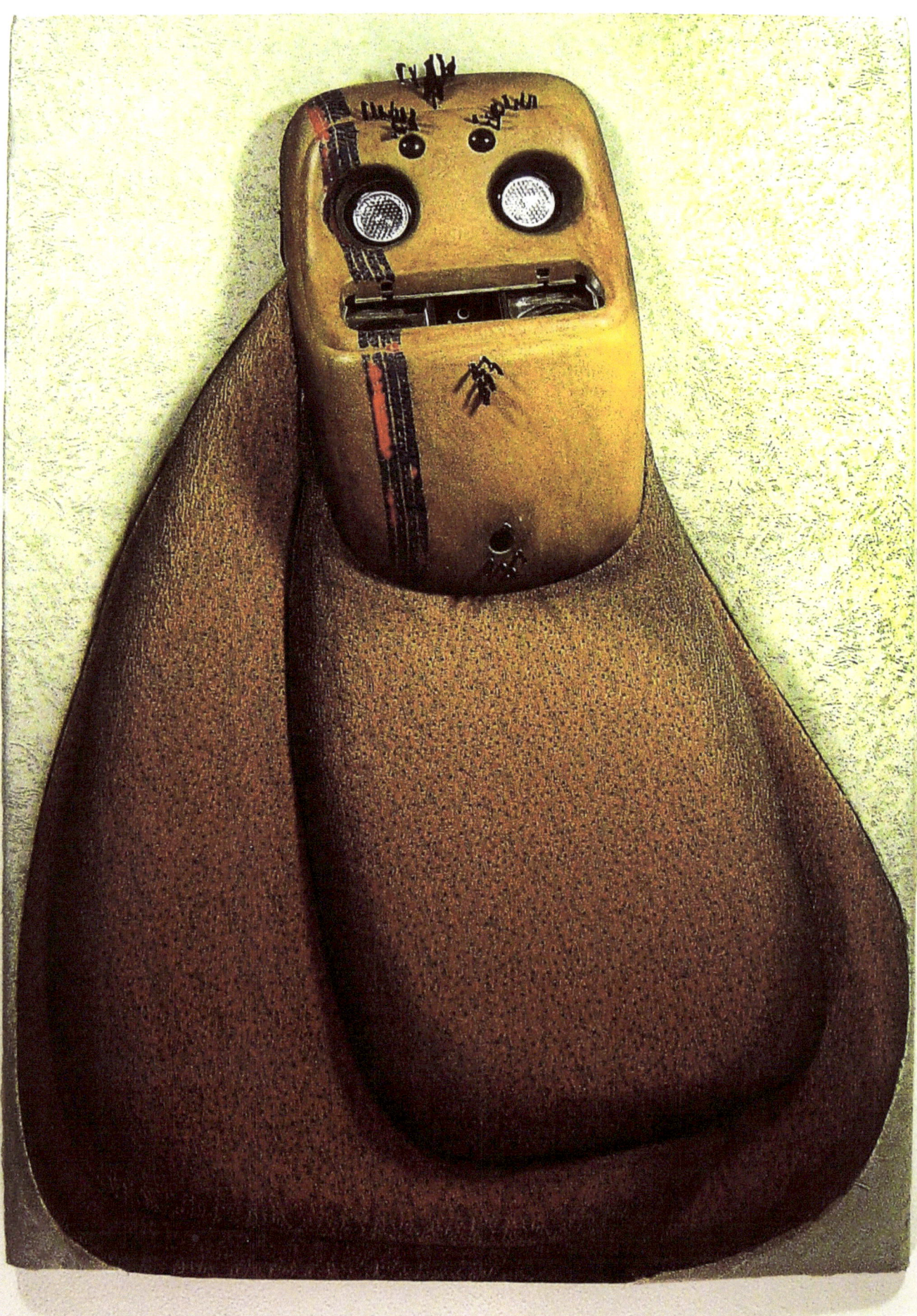

Appetite

Oh yes, we have an appetite all right. After all, we must eat to live, right? But we develop an appetite for foods that will ruin our health, we develop appetites for activities that will wreck our balance and suspend any activity that could be considered spiritual. We are not only talking about our trips to the fridge, but to the internet porn site, and the shopping mall, the TV. How mockingly appropriate is the term "download" like a massive amount of stuff, pouring into an already burdened carrier. It strains and groans under the new burden of stuff, unwieldy and difficult now to climb a hill, so difficult to maneuver because of the shear mass of……….
….all the available things we crave.

Our American world is so chocked full of stuff for us to crave that most of us bear multiple versions of excess appetite. Then it comes time to seek a living God, to come before Him to partake of his wisdom, and who are we? What do we bring?   He wants us with nothing and we show up so laden with the excess of our consumption that we do not know how to even seek his presence.

Fasting is not very fashionable. But it may be one of the only ways to even recognize what habits we have constructed for ourselves, and how severely they get in between us and a relationship to a living God who's life is the light of men. Like Pavlov's dog we respond to the bell on cue, we salivate on command just like Madison Avenue wants us to.   Ah, so well trained, is it nicotine, alcohol, sweets, or sex? Do we know how it started and what should be considered normal?   And worst of all, when we come before Him, can we be apart from our craving long enough to enter in? How often should we enter in? There are few natural curbs for appetites in our modern culture, we may have to create our own.

What is in Your worship?

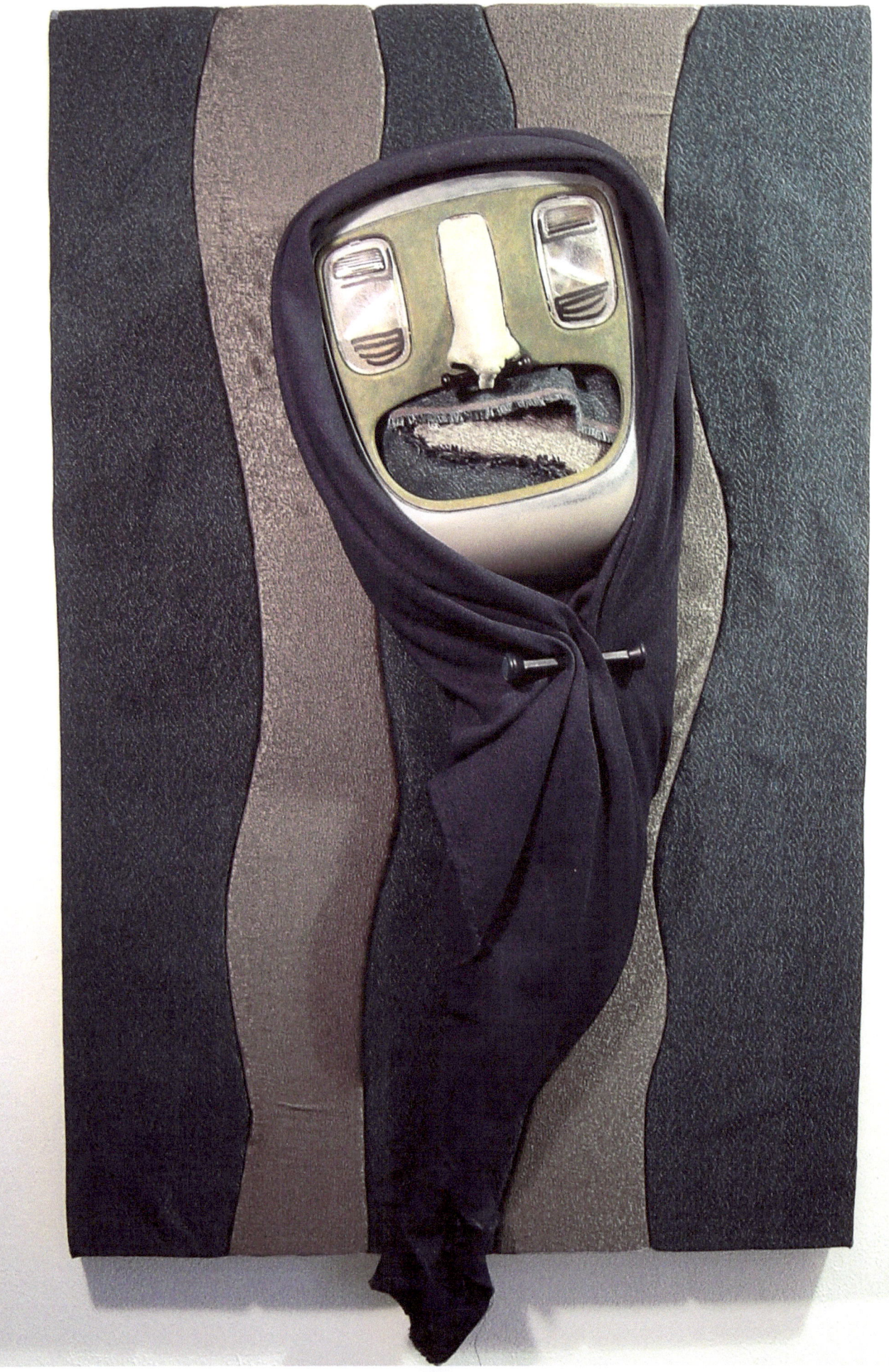

Persistence of Memory

We are the sum total of our memories, so we seem to think.
What has happened to us is what our consciousness is built around. But when we come to the task of spiritual interaction there is an eternal soul that is barely scratched by the time we have spent here in this life. Our creation by a perfect Creator to interact with Him in an absolutely unique way is usually not what comes to mind when we think of our past.

Some of us bear the tremendous scars of abuse, rejection, ridicule. Some have had incredible love, and fantastic wealth of friendship, happiness or an endeavor, and lost it. Some times we dwell on the most miniscule happening at some tender age imagining every other person on the planet sees this incident written all over us.

We dwell on these things. The stuff from our past comes floating in to our consciousness like little familiar ghosts at all manner of odd times. Whether good or bad it can consume an inordinate amount of time. Some dwell exclusively here and descend into self medication for relief.

If we come to worship we come to an eternal being, with the power to recreate us in less of an instant than it took Him to consider our original creation. One who has an infinite number of patterns available for our make-over. One who resides in the midst of only purity. If we come to Him at all, bearing scars from our past, he is pleased. If we come and ask for release from these impediments to comprehending the eternal destiny which we can enter into, He hears.
But we look to the past. If we bend backwards looking behind, from an upside down perspective, out of balance, we eventually fall over.
We are simply not designed to be in that position.

God can release us from any level of past and allow us to look forward with increasing hope and expectation…. if we ask. When these memories slip in to our worship we need to bring them to Him who has reconciled all of it, and count it our strength to have been tested.

What is in Your Worship?

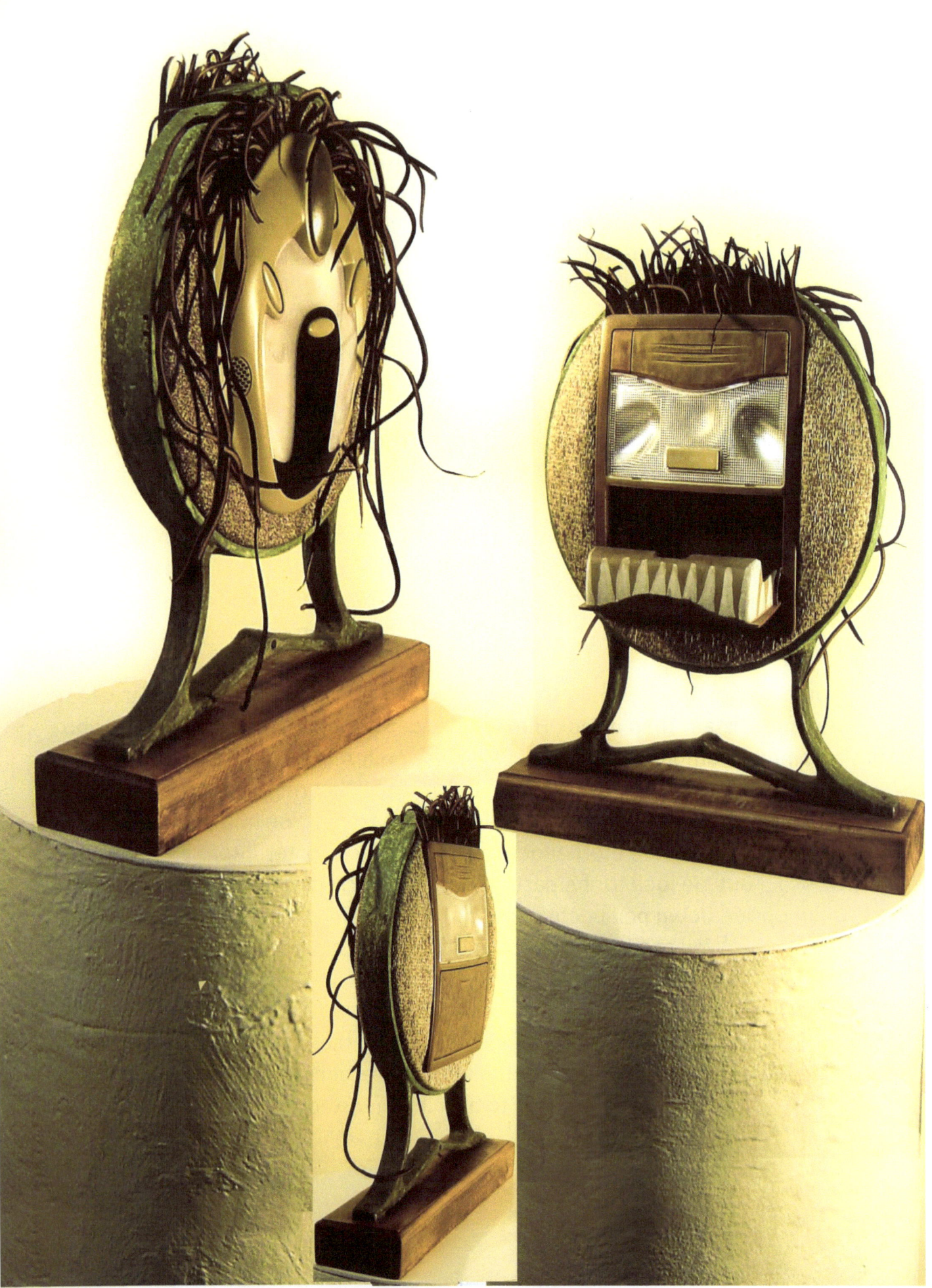

Medusa Max

Under great stress we can freak out inside and almost become like the famed mythological Medusa, so bitter that we want to turn others to stone. The slithering snake haired goddess is much like our frustration that can make us lash out at others. Do we focus on our condition so hard that we become a lashing demon? The human condition can be altered by something as little as a bad hair day. Has the serpent gotten in your head?

What's in Your Worship?

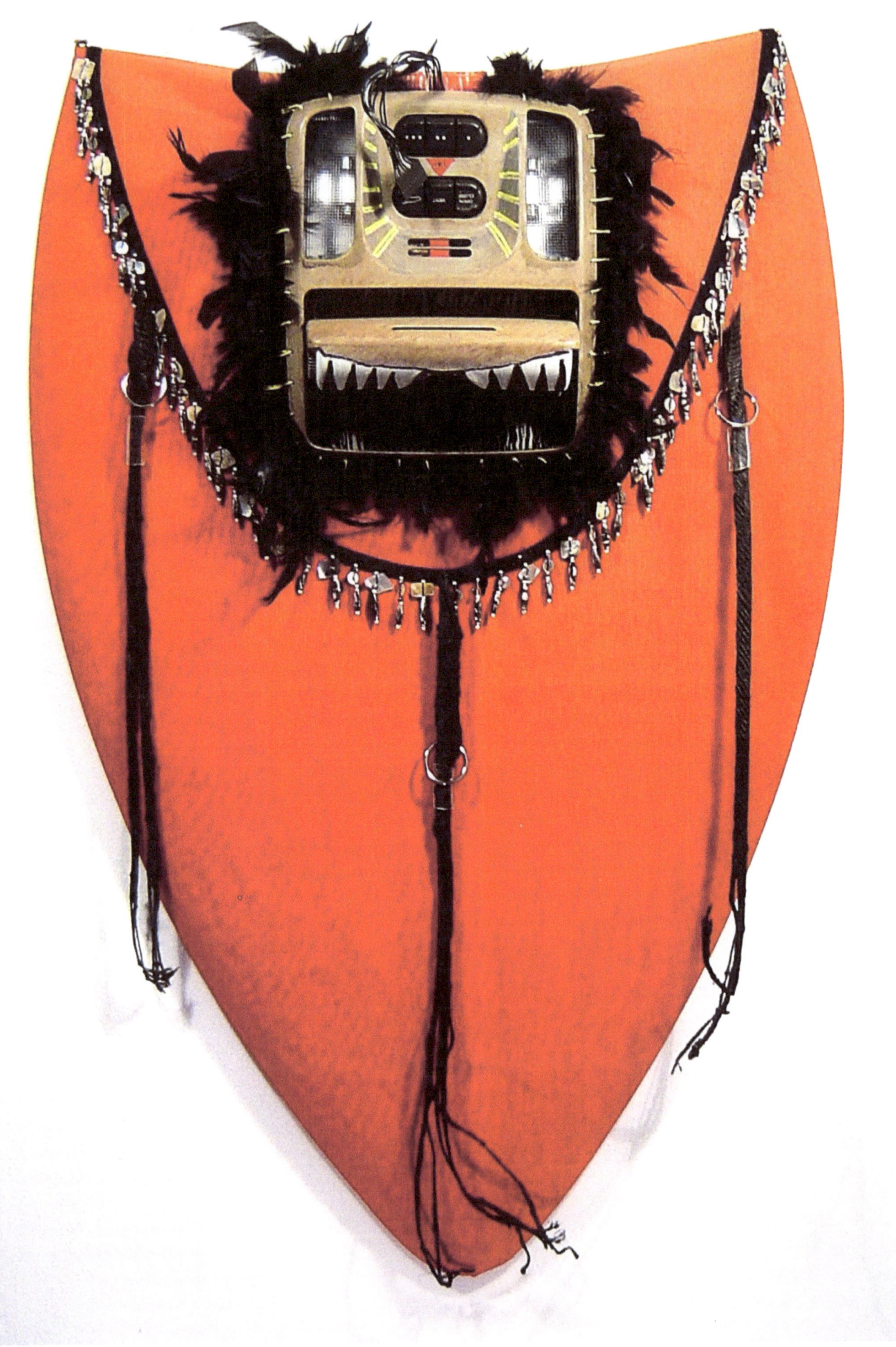

Shielded Heart

We shield our hearts from everything, we defend our pumping blood and the deepest cores of our very lives from contact with anything that could go too deep and cause us harm.   Any extraction is too costly, so don't risk it, better to keep this defended.

Our Spouses and children certainly belong there. But so do our extended families, and our neighbors too, according to the commandment, if we are to love. But we fill our hearts with the distractions of our world as well. Slowly we come to love our home, our car, our ball team, our careers, our work. Soon our entire heart can be so full of stuff that we want no more.

If we have experienced loss, we know heart break and heart ache. This experience builds calluses. *" Let's not let that happen again. Man, too painful".* As we have a few bad experiences we begin to shield this heart from anything that might pierce, and only let in what we know to be safe. Then we focus on those nice safe ones. Or worse case, we grow so callous that we harbor evil in there and have **no room for compassion** or any extension toward another soul who may be presented to us with a need. And most of us can become so mesmerized by our mundane loves that there is no real space for the Holy Spirit of God. We come to our efforts of worship, hearts too filled with the rest to extend it, to open it to our loving father God who knows all about how these other things have affected us.   It takes a concerted effort to unchain the shield we construct and let Him in there to heal and strengthen our life's blood. It is so difficult to remember that He is the source of this very life that courses through at the pumping of the organ.

What's in Your Worship?

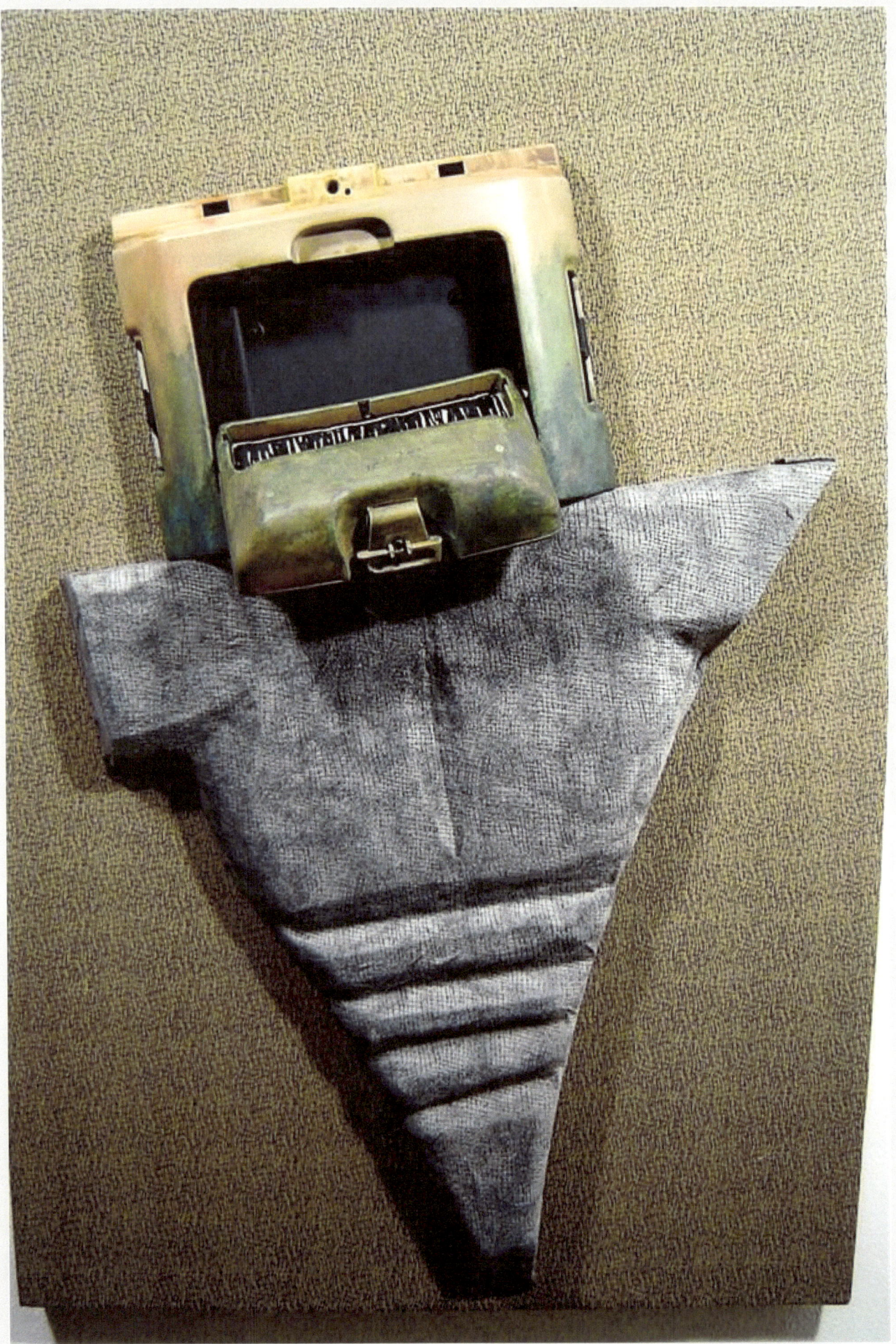

The Body Buffet

The all powerful focus on the flesh, it is of course how we gauge the state of our life. "Are we healthy?" is a very good question. And of course the request for healing is a sound reason to come before the Master. But He also tells us not to focus on the flesh. Our society truly places physique in the category of worship. There is so much attention paid to our sex/youth culture that we cannot really avoid its influence. We all prefer to be attractive, and the statistics prove the advantage this has in the career markets. But what of this as we come to a time to seek out God? What must we do to negate the incredible focus on bod-beautiful as we come before Him? Have we got the discipline to turn this stuff off when we come?

And if we suffer from a lack in this area what then? Or damage, or a million other "abnormalities" that grow larger in number as our definition of perfection narrows the bell curve? What then of our time with Him? Our focus can be consumed, can be all on the physical and even worse, all on our personal physical obsessions. We are weak but he is strong. And one who has endured physical testing of disease, or decay, or any manor of sub-desirable condition and still come through to Him with an indomitable spirit that soars to his heart --these are the blessed in deed.

If the rich man has difficulty with the kingdom of heaven I would think the beautiful one has close to the same amount of struggle.

What's in your Worship?

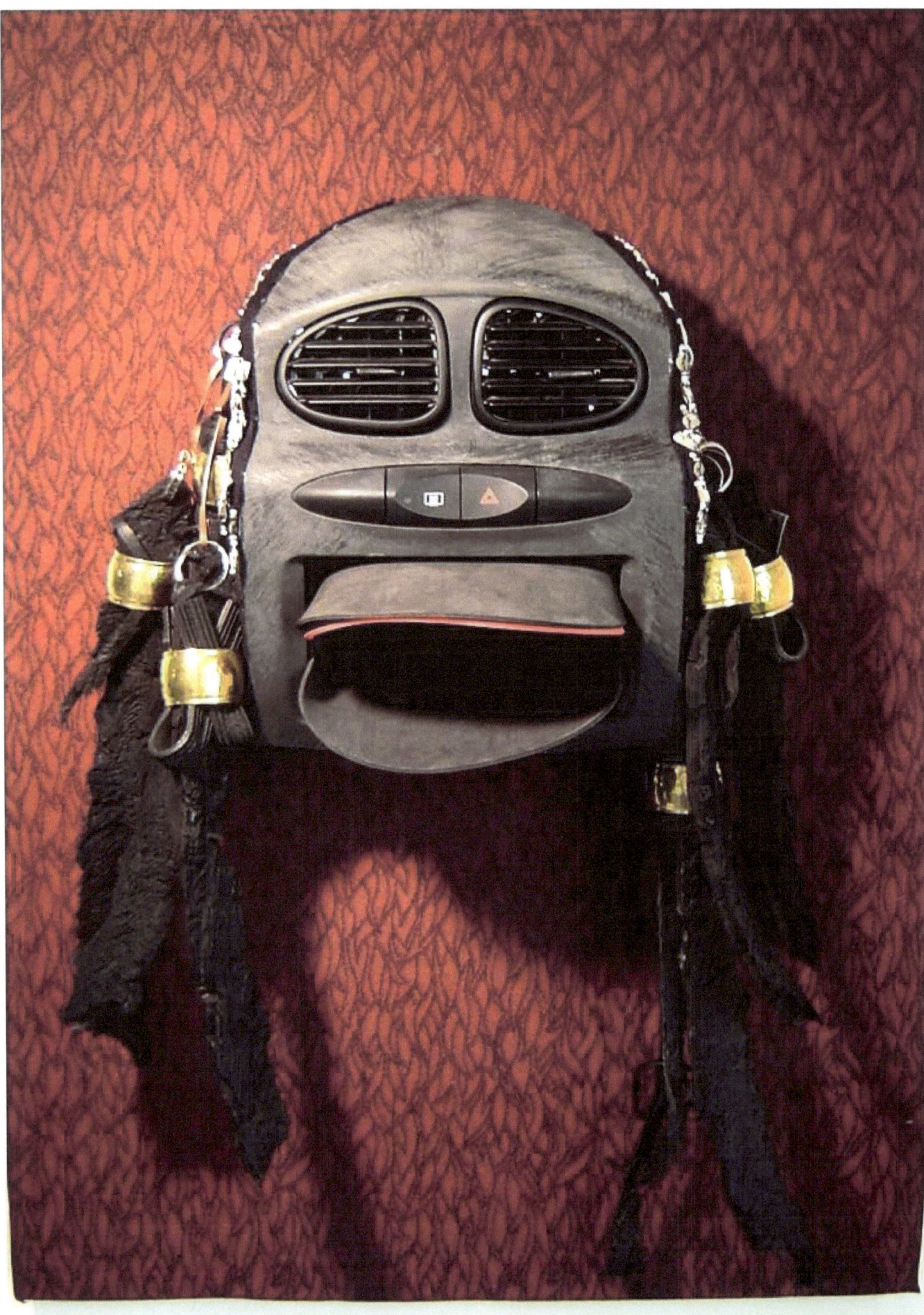

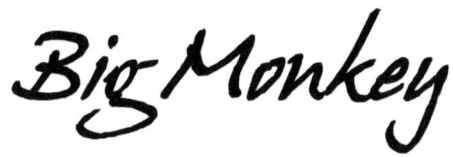

Big Monkey

What do you call an 800 pound gorilla?   Sir.

That is the old joke. We all carry a certain number of monkeys. They are things that must get done. Some larger than others. Just respect for them, and their magnitude, does not deal with them. Business management texts tell us to beware what monkeys we actually accept on our shoulders and which ones we hand off to others. They seem imperative to success and drive us, consuming our mind. They are dangerous, putting careers and objectives in peril if not satisfied. Watching a big one we note a quick twitch of that head and a focused grunt in our direction bodes a possible lashing out of those powerful limbs.

What if this sucker jumped on me?!

We know the scene of an ape's tirade, so violent and noisy. So how do you carry your personal monkeys? Is there a particularly big one at the moment? Like all the rest of the creatures in this world these things are predictable and can be subjugated by the man or woman who grasps the difference between them and us. All these were made to populate the world that you and I inhabit. But we were created to cultivate this place. We were first given the task of naming these beasts, then tending them. When we come to our maker we bring with us our tendency to be concerned for our various tasks, but they should not rule us. They should not drive the spiritual relationship. Each of these will pass, along with our concern for them, even the 800 pounders. And yet our time with God will remain.

Do not let the primates of your life run you, or you risk skipping the real power for their tending.

What's in your Worship?

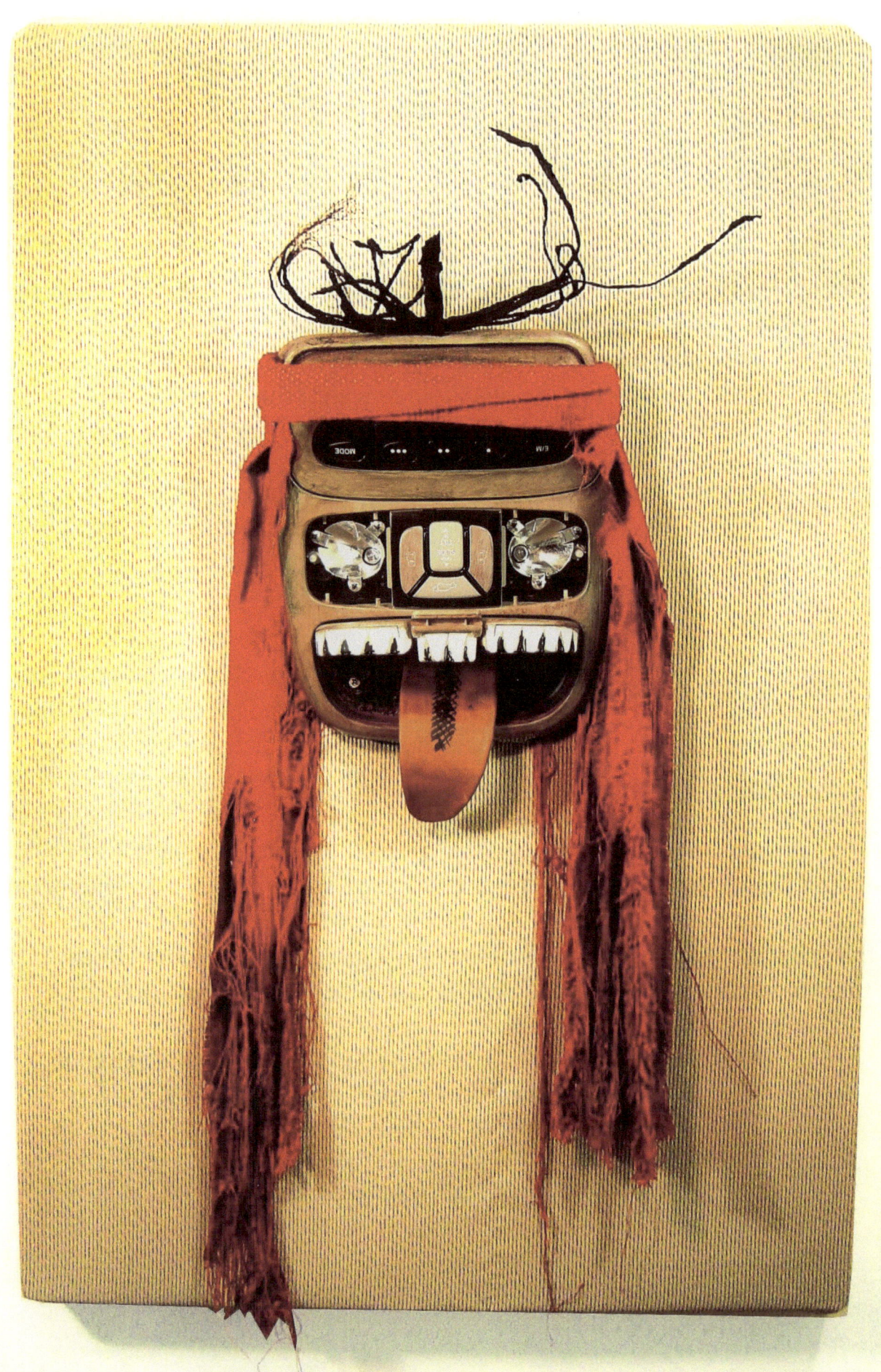

That Comment

How are you dressed? Are you concerned with what others think?
Feel that you may be out of style, fashion, inappropriately dressed? Did you hear
someone comment about your attire? As you see others what comes to mind?   You
may find yourself formulating comments in your mind about how others are dressed:
"Suit and tie -he is trying hard to impress," "baseball hat in the building, obviously no
manners and not a professional. Does he hide a bald spot?" "Torn stockings, can't she
afford to keep those kids dressed?" The list goes on and on and we all do it, judging
those around us and fearing their judgments in return. As a friend once prayed:
*"Forgive me Lord for what I am thinking and thank you for not letting it come out of
my mouth!"*

We were designed by God to be observant, and make judgments and discernments in
order to cultivate his garden. This means spotting places for improvements, and
planning actions to make them happen. But "the fall" gave us the twisted air of
superiority and the fear of inferiority. Both these states translate into our bizarre
obsession with our clothing and the insidious little game of words on the topic. How
often when we stand to seek God we merely dwell on the comments made about us,
or those we would make about others. It is a little obsession, but for some people it
grows into an all consuming and total obstruction to a state of presence with God. Do
you desire to be seated in the place of honor? It is not your attire that will get you
there.

Consider the very first clothing; fig leaves, quick covering from embarrassment. And
the next set? God slew animals and made them of skin, introducing the concept of
death to Adam and Eve in the making of the garments.
We have not changed in all these generations.

From the 6th chapter of Mathew V 25:

*Therefore I tell you, do not worry about your life...what you will wear. Is not life more important than
food, and the body more important than clothes? And why do you worry about clothes? See how the
lilies of the field grow. They do not labor or spin. Yet I tell you that not even Solomon in all his splendor
was dressed like one of these. If that is how God clothes the grass of the field, which is here today and
tomorrow is thrown into the fire, will he not much more clothe you, O you of little faith? So do not
worry, saying….. 'What shall we wear?' For the pagans run after all these things, and your heavenly
Father knows that you need them. But seek first his kingdom and his righteousness, and all these
things will be given to you as well.*

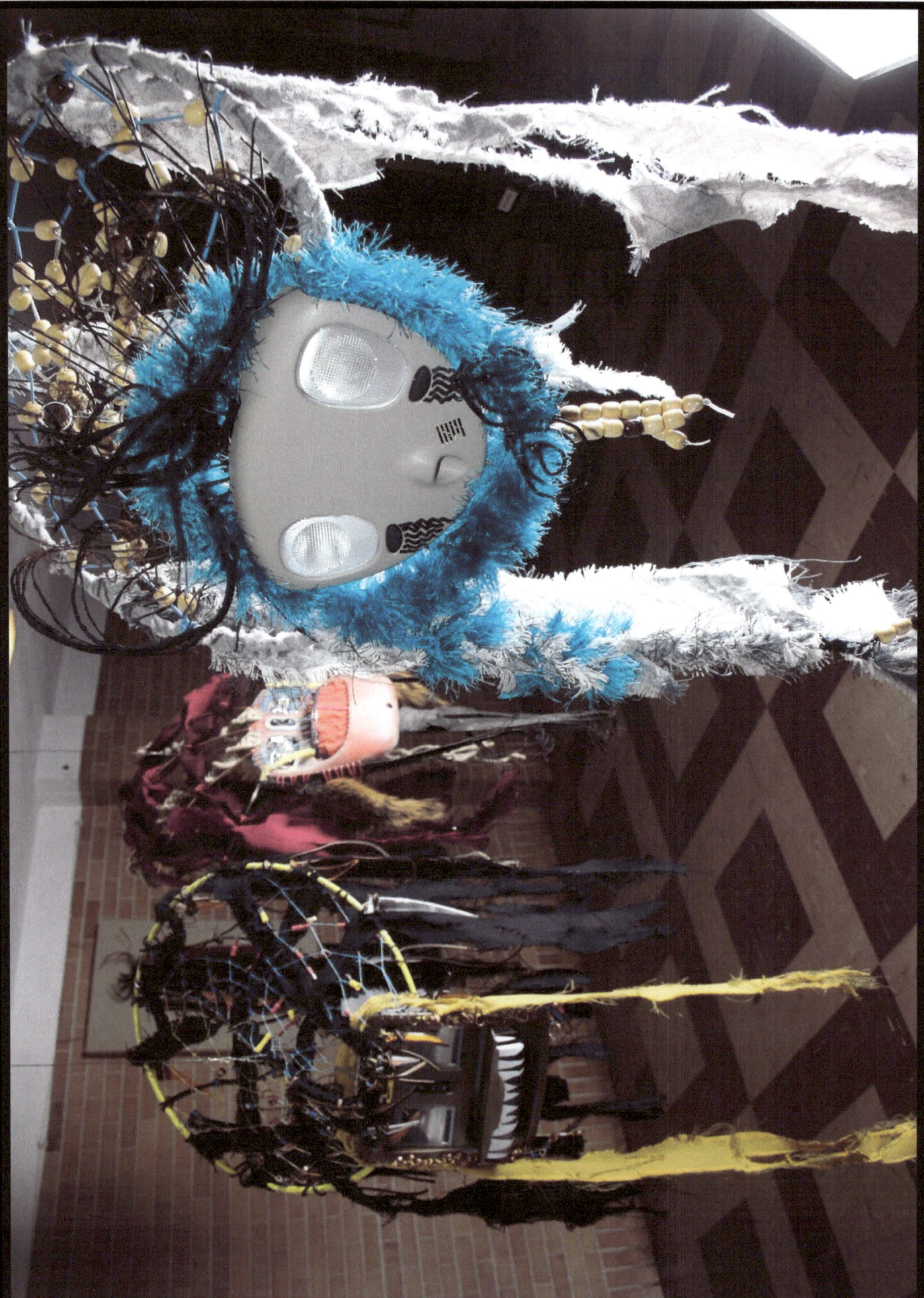

Anger &Embarrassment Tempered with Self Pity

These three were assembled together as a mobile. They slowly float by each other circumspect and leering. Just as our minds migrate from one of these to another in our states of distress. They come with us most often. We bring them separately and often we bring them, all together. Often they can be intertwined because they are the most common in our interactions with others and with our spiritual walk. They can crowd out real communication with God.

"Don't Let the sun set on your anger" not easy.

"There is no condemnation in Christ Jesus" but we are still embarrassed for our gaffs.

"Oh woe is me, I'm such a.... (fill in the blank)" now we introspect hoping God will notice, but then what? Self pity is at least not focused on others but it is still in the way of a communication with God.

What's in Your Worship?

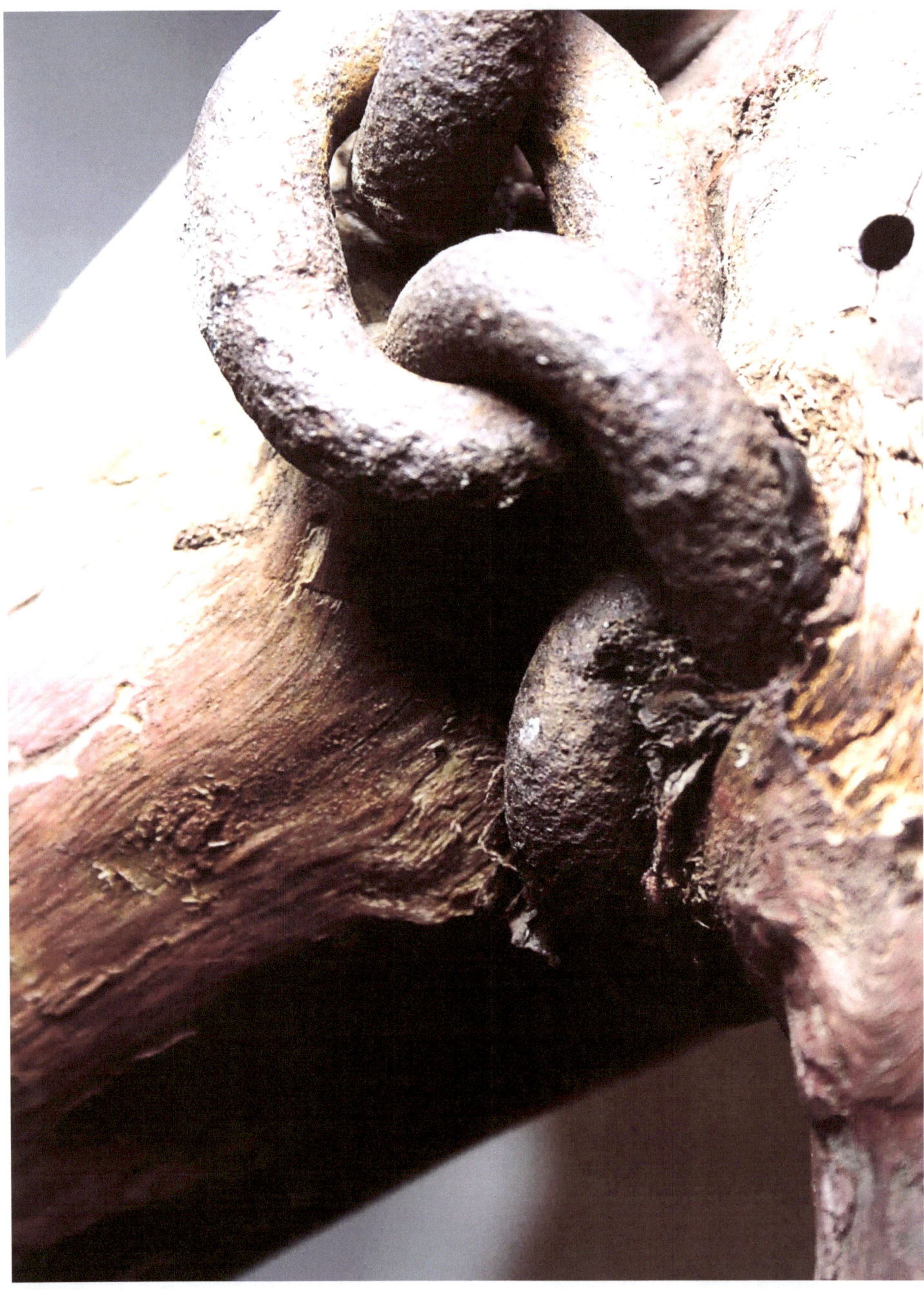

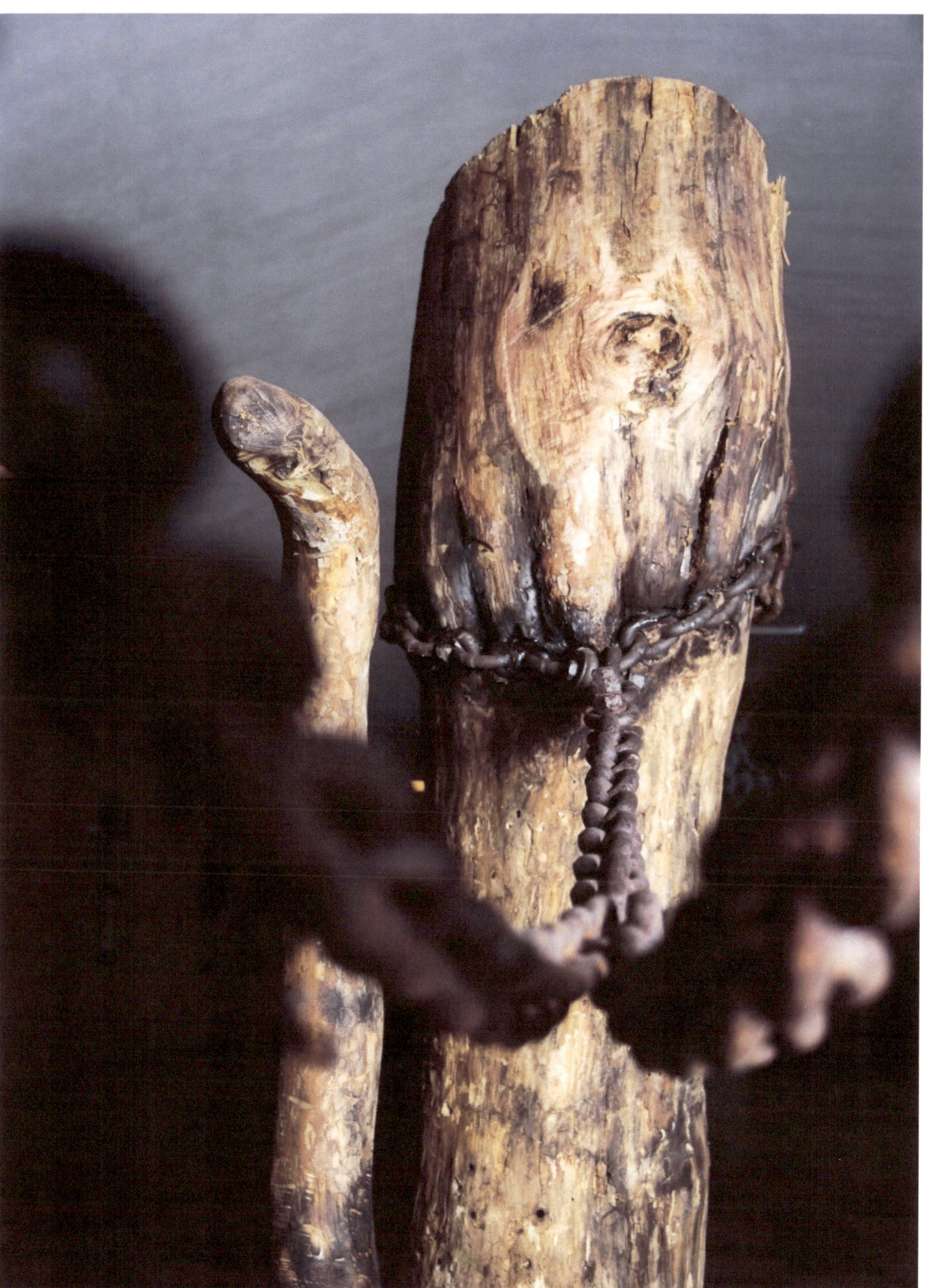

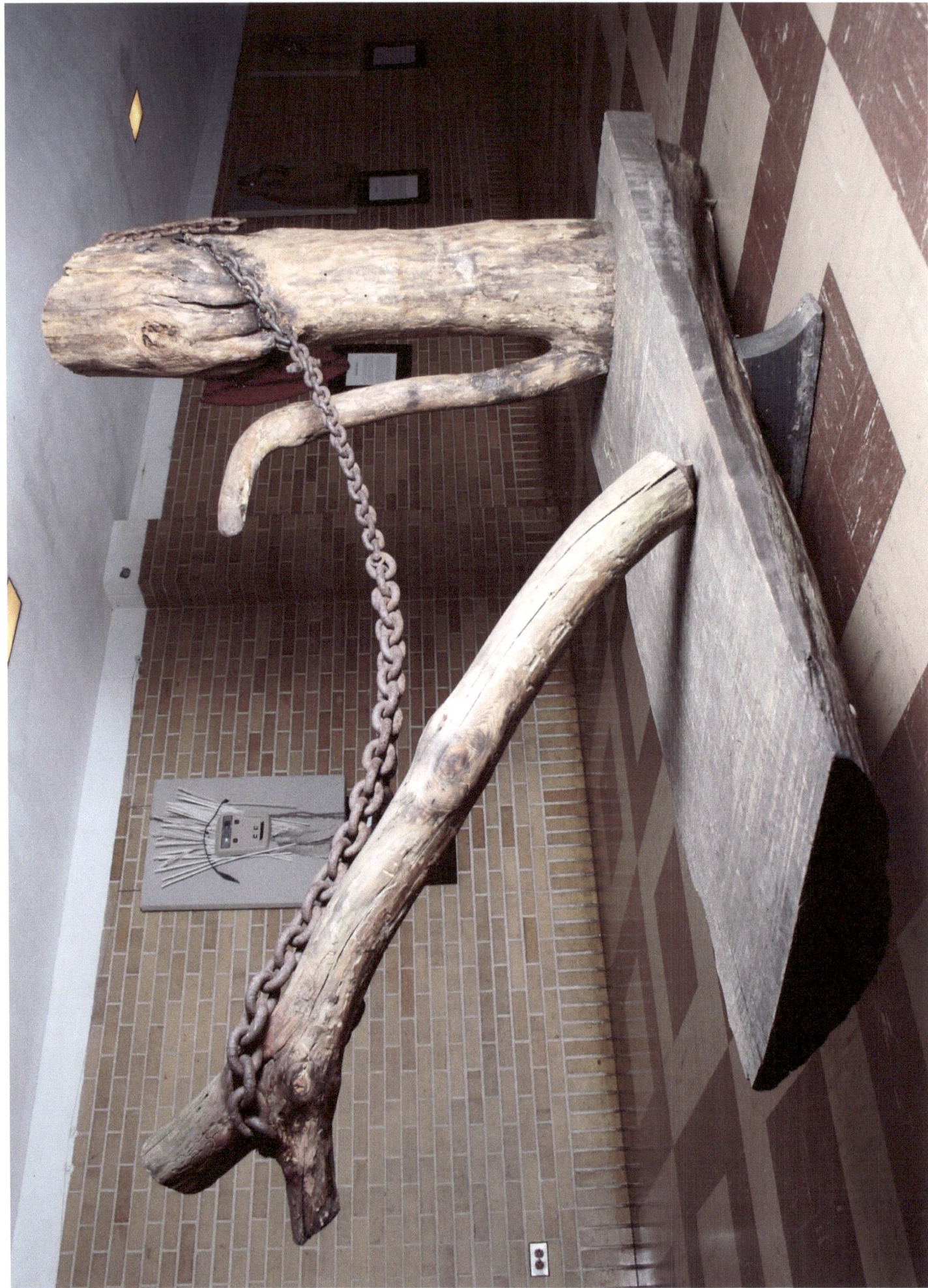

Ancient Constraints

They keep us from growth, prevent our free association with the higher spiritual power and bind us tightly to our past errors and old habits. The accuser points our attention to them, We cannot possibly be worthy.

The old book calls it sin. The new book says it's paid.

What's in your Worship?

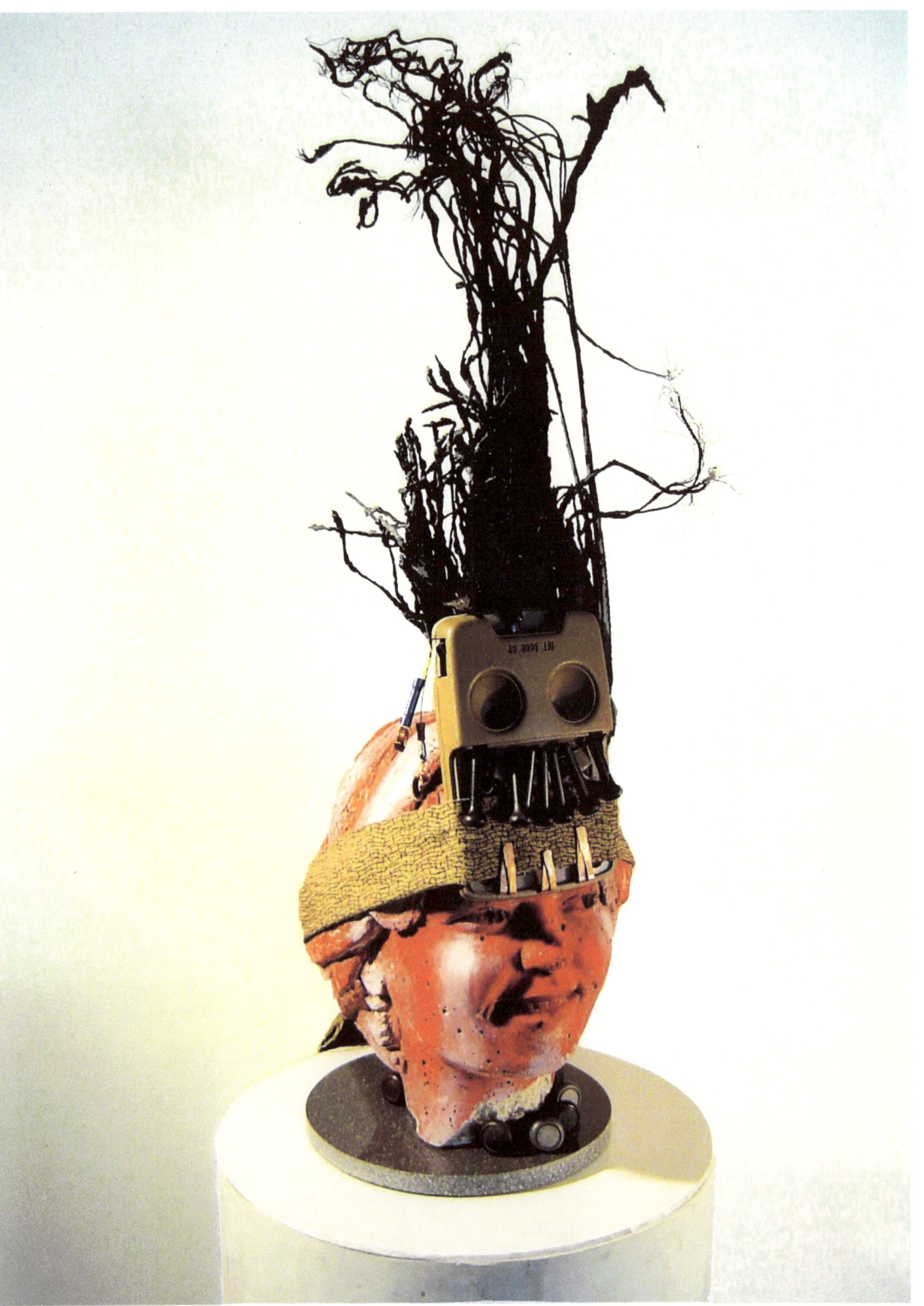

Inner Child 2

How have we been branded by our youthful experiences? Do we wear a sign on our forehead (make an L with a hand). Does our Peter Pan wildness show up and drive us into things we know better than getting into?

No matter to the Master. Regardless of how naughty we have been, how ragged and ashamed of our early path we have become, He understands. Yeah we had to do some things to survive and some others have suffered from our careless actions, but He gets it. After all Christ was born homeless and hunted for his life by authorities while still a babe. Can you imagine the tricks He could play as a boy?

He gets you. We have to acknowledge that inner child before we can step across the spiritual threshold that brings the great peace. The inner child does not melt away but instead becomes stronger for the knowledge of a true need for guidance, and a place to get it.

What's in your Worship?

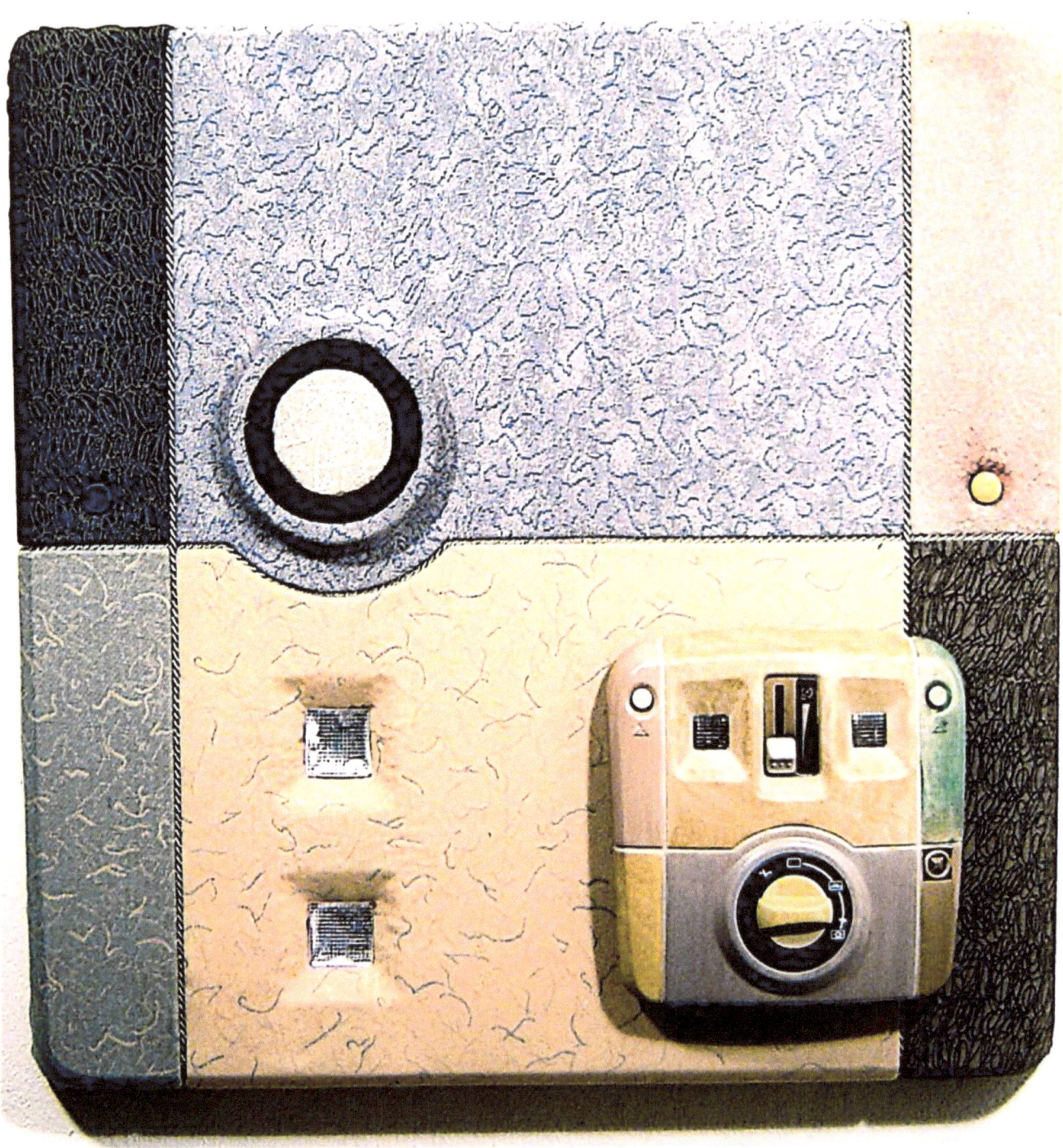

Analytic Camouflage

How bright we can be.

Yes, in our modern society we have come to understand psychology, to grasp the lessons of history and weigh current events against the past plodding of our forefathers. And our physical science –mercy, we have mastery of so much biology that we can do a heart transplant, and calculate the requirements to send a man to the moon and bring him back again. Yes the modern man is so much more sophisticated than before. We no longer merely cultivate gardens, we have landscape architects for beauty and our mass production agriculture has GPS controlled nutrient application and yield calculation. We can gather knowledge at the touch of a button on the web. And we can find out the wind speed of an approaching storm.

All this capability can make us so full of ourselves. We can come to the master of all that we are learning about and try our mind functions on Him. We can assess the odds of an event taking place and try to figure out where the resources most likely can or will come from. *We can apply all we know to the point of missing all that He is.* Our capacity to think is the same as those who came before us, but the subjects for us to apply them to are many more, and better organized. What does this do to our relationship with Him? That depends on what you do. You can analyze the position of God for eternity and never discover a thing that was not known by Adam. He experienced Him before the nasty little introduction of our very self-awareness that makes us think we can be like God. All the assessment in the world is merely another form of fig leaf. In the cool of the morning when we go to walk with Him and try to converse with Him we better leave it all behind. Lest He call out your name "Where are you?"

What's in your Worship?

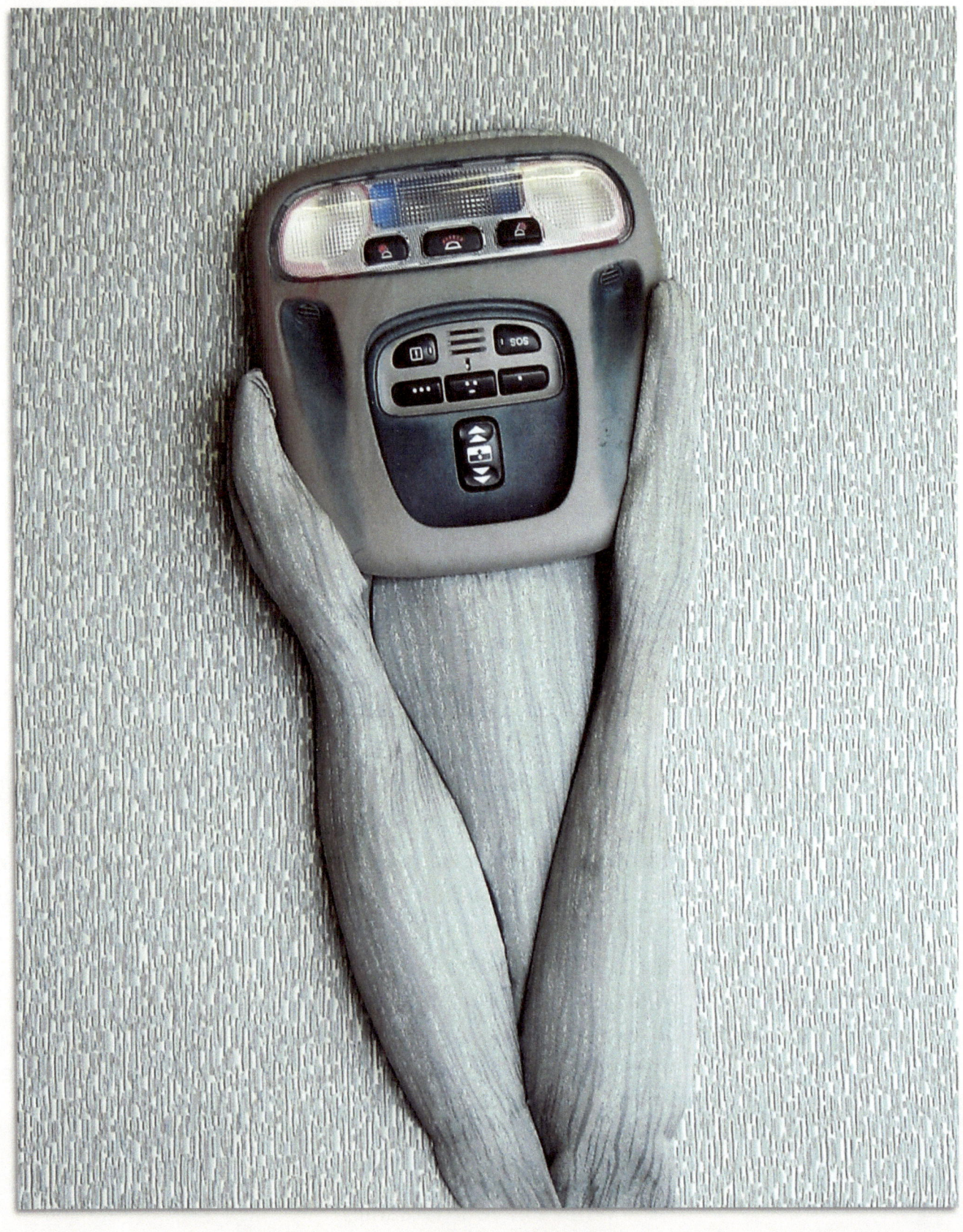

The Silent Scream

We often bear, inside, a silent anxiety, a muffled scream about our fear. We wouldn't dare let it out, and we do not even give it over to our living God.

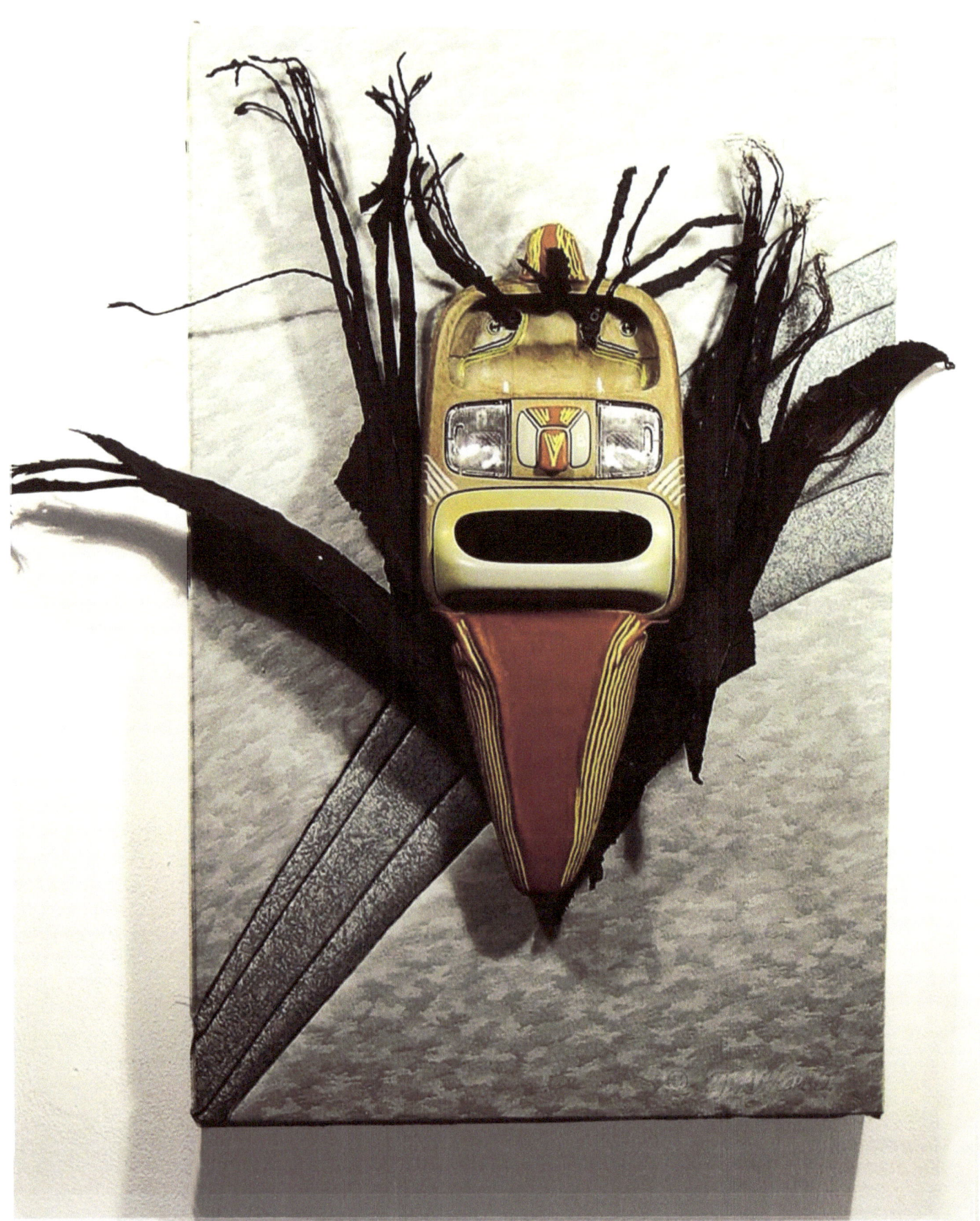

High Flying Expectations

"Oh man, I can't wait to get that thing! I barely slept last night just thinking about how great it is going to be! It will make me so happy, so complete. This is really it , I've wanted this for so long."

Then we get it and within moments we begin to test the truth of those expectations. Then we note the first flaw, then another. If we encounter a major flaw too quickly the shock of disappointment strikes like a rock, pow. What! Oh Crap!

The aerodynamics of our expectations begin to wither. The spiral downward ensues, and as we pass the threshold of negativity. Our opinion of that object of our desire is shattered. The thud of a wasted mass of anticipation is heard hitting ground, softened by cold rain. The parade is over. And we begin the cycle again.

Maybe we learn from the rollercoaster ride, maybe we don't.
Maybe we grow skeptical that anything is achievable, that any object will be true to it's expectation. Maybe we become so sour to anything new that we adopt a bit more vicious version of Eore's litany "It will never work, why bother." No one wants to be the delusional twerp who believes in a hopeless cause and then fakes bits of outcome to bolster his lame mental construct.
Our Maker desires neither unreal fantasy nor skepticism from us. He wants us to come without any of this. Our physical world gives us so many conflicting lessons that we cannot reconcile with an all-powerful spiritual being. So we must approach empty. This is not an amusement ride. Forget the trestles and the launching devices. There are no seat- belts either, just Him and you and all that He is which is not comprehendible to our mortal selves. The Highest of our expectations are specks of dust to him, and the greatest disappointments are rectified by his mere glance in eternity.

What's in Your worship?

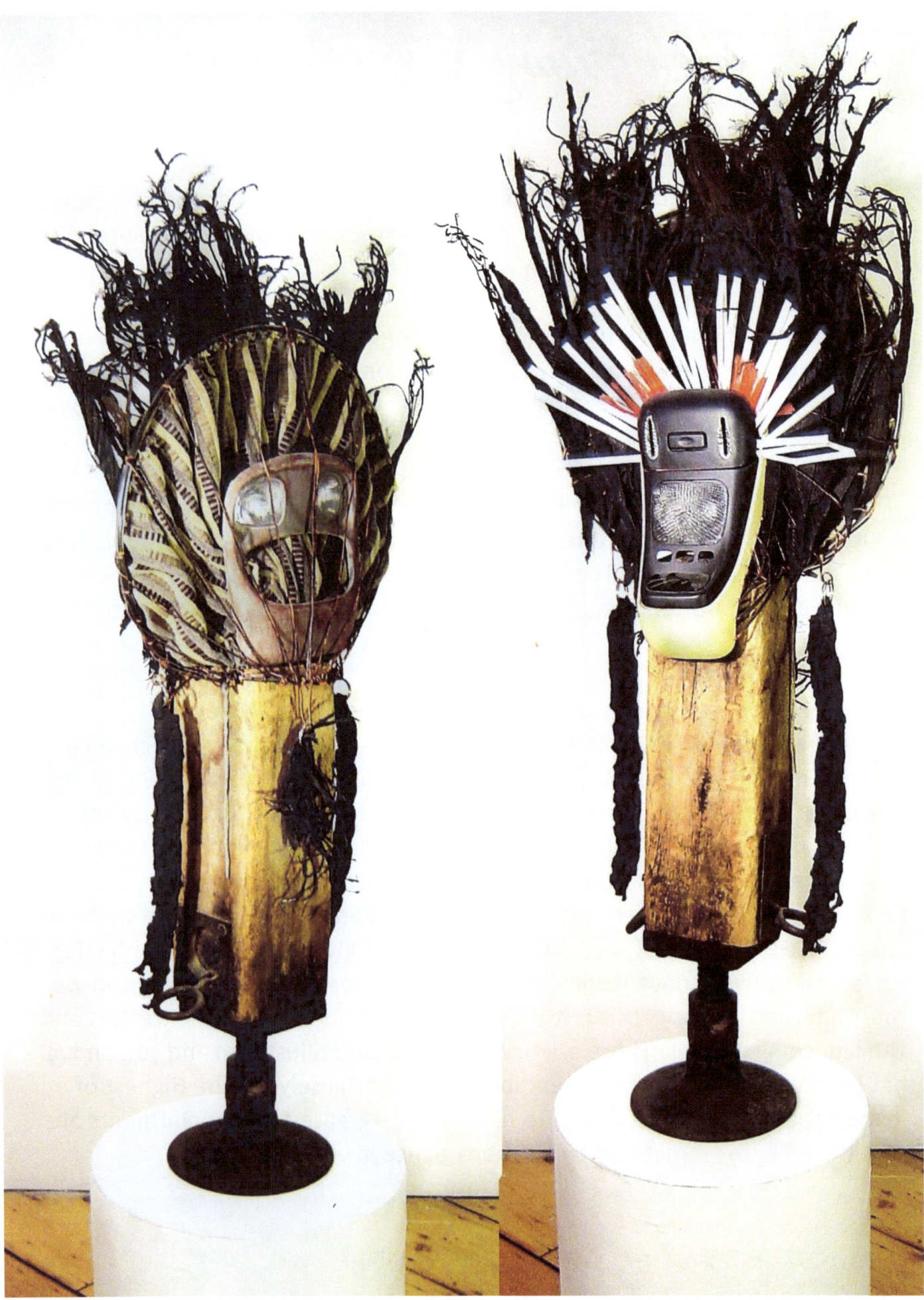

Dual Minded Man

One side pokes out at the space with high contrast but has no mouth. The other side is caged in, mouth open but no depth of statement can happen with that mouth. This piece swivels on it's base and can easily turn from one side to the other.

   When we come seeking God, He may speak to us, but our double nature holds us from accepting his word. What is our true response to his prompting? We often are in denial that we even have a problem with what God is trying to tell us. We avoid His truths if they don't fit our past experience, or if they seem too simple or hurtful. We want it our way, but we hope it's His way, and faced with the difference we can't decide, so we vacillate.

   How often we just slowly wander away from Him in a moment of his speaking. We may not even realize that we are in denial of His position. Our double mindedness prevents us from going deeper, and we stay at our current level or slide backwards, to reticent too accept his perfect will.

What's in Your worship?

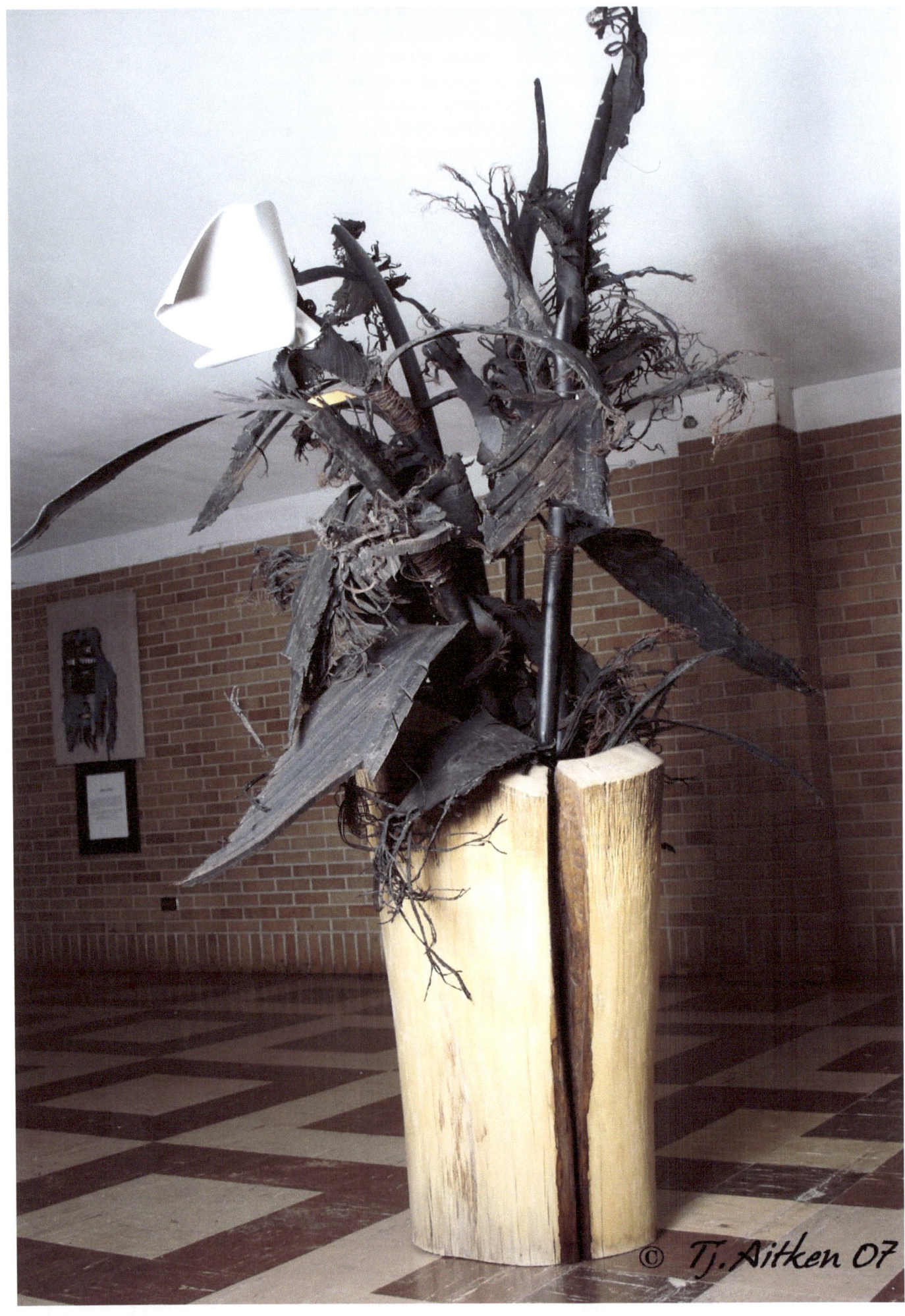

© Tj.Aitken 07

Imperfect Vessel

At first glance it is a vase with floral arrangement. But as we get closer they are not plants at all but pieces of shredded tires and old tubes. The wood is split and stained, weeping. And this thing is large. If you get to close the steel barbs will grab your hair or clothing. Like all our acquaintances none of us is fit to be in the presence of God, and barely fit to interact with each other. Our flaws are massive and our personal lives a knarly mess that no one wants to get into. In this state we come to Him, yet he provides a way to communicate if we do indeed recognize our personal state.
We have the Son to thank for reconciliation.

What's in your Worship?

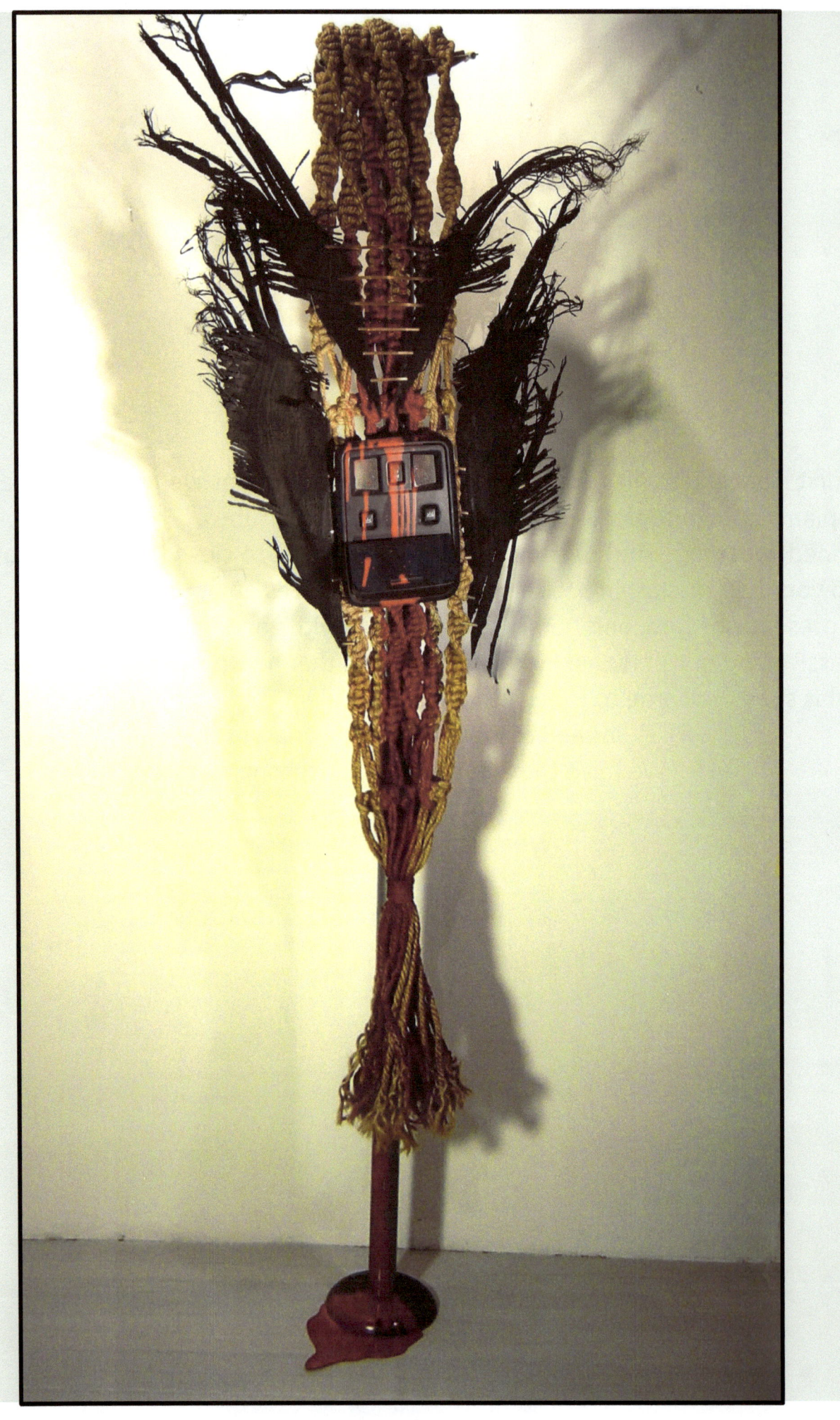

Unforgiveness

Probably the single most inexcusable infringement on our spiritual condition is holding a grudge against someone. The presence of our desire to see that individual harmed is an insidious evil. It floats about in our consciousness and is barely noticeable. We can go for years with hardly a thought of the original infraction, then suddenly it is there before us with fangs, seeking blood.

What is unforgivable to you? Time heals all wounds. Is this true? Here we are as forgiven souls with a free pass to eternal life and we hold something against another soul? These festering situations can lead to bitterness. Bitterness will make us actually look ugly over time, and so change our life that few will take pleasure in our presence.

Have you been wronged? Let it be known … and then let it go. It is not worth the distance it puts between you and a compassionate God.

Consider this story ending:
'I canceled all that debt of yours because you begged me to. Shouldn't you have had mercy on your fellow servant just as I had on you?' In anger his master turned him over to the jailers to be tortured, until he should pay back all he owed. "This is how my heavenly Father will treat each of you unless you forgive your brother from your heart." Mathew 32- 35

What's in *Your* Worship?

A portion of the proceeds from this book go to help Chronic Lyme sufferers through the Lyme Disease United Coalition that helps hundreds with their medical bills.

Sculpture by Tj Aitken, with thanks to Mereta Kies, WoW Vineyard, Holland MI. Photos by Tj and Ryan Shine
Copies available at www. SculptureByTj.com

Video animations on these works, along with other Books By Tj are available at SculptureByTj.com

"Art Savvy"-(a field guide to understanding modern sculpture)
Big Sculpture for Little series:
Scaling up
Carving Foam
Stone Coating

www.ingramcontent.com/pod-product-compliance
Lightning Source LLC
Chambersburg PA
CBHW050813180526
45159CB00004B/1653